National Trust
Book of
Scones

National Trust
Book of
Scones

Sarah Clelland

First published in the United Kingdom in 2017 by
National Trust Books
43 Great Ormond Street
London
WC1N 3HZ

An imprint of Pavilion Books Group Ltd

ISBN: 9781909881938

A CIP catalogue record for this book is available from the
British Library.

20 19
12

Reproduction by Mission, Hong Kong
Printed and bound by 1010 Printing Internation Ltd, China

This book can be ordered direct from the publisher at the website:
www.pavilionbooks.com, or try your local bookshop. Also available
at National Trust shops or www.nationaltrustbooks.co.uk.

Contents

Introduction

In February 2013, two things happened: I turned thirty-nine and I joined the National Trust. Other people in my position would have thought 'I'll hit forty this time next year, I'm off on a hedonistic rampage' and gone to Ibiza for twelve months. Not me. It's for the best: I'm not making a fool of myself in nightclubs, and now we have a nice sticker on our windscreen.

We joined at Chartwell – even with my terrible maths, I could see that joining and getting access to 500+ places was better than paying to visit one – and I was very excited about it. But months went by and no second outing took place. And when I did finally travel the massive 1½ miles from my house to Osterley Park in London, I enjoyed it immensely but couldn't remember anything about it when I got home.

And so I formed a mission: I would travel to every National Trust place. At each one, I would record the most fascinating bits of its history and I would reward myself with a scone. And so the National Trust Scone blog, featuring reviews of both properties and their scones, was born.

Since then, I have visited a lot of National Trust properties. I can tell you that my affection for the Trust has grown and grown. Each property has its own story – whether it's Moseley Old Hall where Charles II hid under the floorboards, or Clouds Hill where Lawrence of Arabia wrote before his fatal motorbike accident just up the road. Nothing makes me happier than knowing I'm going on a little roadtrip to see where Agatha Christie lived, or Anne Boleyn was probably born, or the house at Lyme that stood in for Pemberley in *Pride & Prejudice* (very popular place for marriage proposals, that last one).

As for the scones – my love for those has grown as well. Having eaten 150+ so far, I can let you into the secret of a good one: it has to be freshly baked. It doesn't really matter what recipe you follow (though the official National Trust one used by their cafés is included in this book and comes highly recommended), and it doesn't matter whether you call them 'scons' or 'sc-owns', or if you put jam or cream on first – if they are fresh, it takes a lot to ruin a scone.

That's why I am *delighted* that you are the owner (or borrower) of this book. These recipes will ensure that you never run out of ideas for a teatime treat, and if you bake and eat them within a couple of hours, you can't go wrong.

Happy sconeing!

Principles of Scones

Use medium eggs unless otherwise stated

Use whole (full-fat) milk unless otherwise stated

All spoon measurements level unless otherwise stated

Standard spoon measures: 1 tsp = 5ml (5g); 1 tbsp = 15ml (15g)

Oven temperatures are for conventional ovens. If you use a fan oven you may need to reduce the temperature by 10°C.

The recipes in this book give instructions for making scones by hand. You may prefer to use a food mixer, especially if you are making larger quantities. The principle is the same whichever way you choose. First you need to distribute the fat evenly throughout the flour: if you are rubbing it in by hand, it's best if the butter (or margarine) is chilled and cut into small cubes (or you could grate the chilled fat directly into the flour); using your fingertips, lightly rub the fat into the flour until the mixture looks like fine crumbs; check that it's mixed evenly by tapping the bowl – any large pieces of fat will rise to the surface. If using a mixer, the fat should be softened before you combine it with the flour. Stir the main ingredient (fruit, cheese, chocolate chips, etc) through the dry mix. Finally, add liquid (milk and/or egg) to bind the mixture to form a soft dough, ready to be rolled out.

Work quickly and lightly throughout. Use a light touch if you are mixing and kneading by hand; if using a food mixer, do not overwork the mixture.

A scone mixture should always include a raising agent: many recipes use self-raising flour, which includes a raising agent, but for added height there is no harm in adding another 1 or even 2 teaspoons of baking powder.

Turn the dough out onto a lightly floured surface to prevent it from sticking. When rolling out the dough, don't press hard as this may prevent your scones from rising to fluffy perfection.

When stamping out the scones, push straight down with the cutter, rather than twisting it; this will encourage the scones to rise evenly. To make it easy to lift the cutter cleanly, put some flour into a small bowl and dip the cutter into the flour before stamping out each scone.

The recipes suggest the size of cutter, but use whatever size you like – just bear in mind that small scones will take less time to cook than larger ones, so keep an eye on them as they approach their recommended cooking time so they don't burn.

Choose a baking sheet that's large enough to hold the scones, spaced slightly apart. To prevent your scones from sticking, prepare the baking sheet either by brushing it lightly with butter, margarine or a light cooking oil, or by lining it with greaseproof paper or non-stick baking paper.

Scones need to go into a preheated hot oven: the cooking time is short, so they need to start cooking straight away. Position the shelf just above the centre of the oven.

A good way to tell if the scones are done is to push gently on the top: the scone should feel springy to the touch.

When you take your scones out of the oven, transfer them to a wire rack so they don't sit on the baking sheet – soggy-bottom alert.

Always eat scones fresh, on the day of baking.

The Classics

1

Tintagel Old Post Office (CORNWALL)

If you had to pick one National Trust property that sums up Great Britain, it would surely be Tintagel Old Post Office. You've got Tintagel, the ancient, legendary home of King Arthur. And then you've got the Post Office, with queues stretching for several days across multiple counties. I'm joking about the queues – Tintagel Old Post Office was briefly a post office in Victorian times, so it's not actually open for business today. I did see a man in a stovepipe hat who'd been waiting for a passport application form for 130 years, though.

It was built between 1350 and 1400 and probably began life as the home of a prosperous yeoman. In the 1870s it became the receiving office for letters, but it has also been a grocer's, shoemaker's, draper's and family home. Tintagel began attracting a lot of tourists because of its connections to King Arthur, and as a knock-on (or should that be knock-down?) effect, many buildings were demolished and replaced by hotels.

When the almost derelict Old Post Office came up for auction in 1895, a local artist bought it to preserve it, and the National Trust agreed to buy it from her in 1900. Not surprisingly, it's now a Grade I listed building, with a famously wavy slate roof that looks as though it might collapse at any moment.

It doesn't take long to look round (the Trust recommend you allow an hour), so if you have time to spare you could pop up the road to Tintagel Castle, which is a thoroughly romantic ruin. It's not National Trust, though, so don't tell anyone I recommended it.

Plain Scones

This simple, eggless recipe makes small, light, well-risen scones – perfect served with jam and clotted cream.

350g self-raising flour
50g butter, softened

50g lard, softened
100–115ml milk

Preheat the oven to 190°C. Grease two baking sheets.

Sift the flour into a mixing bowl and rub in the butter and lard, working quickly and lightly, until the mixture resembles fine crumbs. Add enough milk to make a soft, bread-like dough.

On a lightly floured surface, roll out to about 2cm thick and stamp out using a 6cm round cutter. Place on the baking sheets and bake for 15–20 minutes until well risen and lightly golden.

Transfer to a wire rack to cool slightly. Best served while still warm.

2

Killerton (Devon)

Killerton is a very large estate, covering 6,400 acres. The house was built in 1778 for Sir Thomas Acland and remained in the Acland family until it was given to the National Trust.

The last Acland at Killerton was Sir Richard. He was an intriguing man, if a tad indecisive – he was elected as a Liberal MP in 1935 but then became a socialist and formed the Common Wealth Party with J.B. Priestley, then after the Second World War became a Labour MP, before he fell out with them and stood unsuccessfully as an independent. As part of his socialist beliefs, he decided that property should be open to the public and handed Killerton over to the National Trust in 1944. What his four sons made of this is not recorded.

Killerton House itself is quite modest from the outside, but inside it's a nice size with well-proportioned rooms. The Trust encourages visitors to have a go on the piano and organ, which is always good to see (if not hear!). The highlight for me, though, was the Bear Hut in the grounds, which looks a bit like Hagrid's hut in the 'Harry Potter' films. It was originally built as a summerhouse and has a surprisingly dazzling stained-glass window. Each room is lined with unusual materials, from deer skin to pine cones and bark. The floor in the inner room is 'cobbled' with deer knuckle-bones.

When one of the young Aclands brought a bear back from Canada, it took up residence in the hut. The bear was called Tom and there's a replica of him in the ticket office that I can assure you is not nearly as scary as it sounds – when I visited he was wearing a rather fetching hat.

Fruit Scones

The Trust's champion dish; serve with good strawberry jam and generous spoonfuls of clotted cream for the perfect afternoon tea.

450g self-raising flour
115g butter, cubed
85g caster sugar

85g sultanas
1 egg, beaten
200ml milk

Preheat the oven to 200°C. Lightly oil a baking sheet.

Sift the flour into a mixing bowl and rub in the butter, using your fingertips, until it resembles fine crumbs. Stir in the sugar and sultanas.

Add the egg and gradually mix in about 150ml of the milk to make a soft dough.

Turn out the dough onto a lightly floured surface, knead lightly, then roll out to about 2–3cm (two fingers) thick. Stamp out using a 7cm round fluted cutter and transfer to the baking sheet. Knead the trimmings together lightly, re-roll and stamp out more rounds until you have made eight scones.

Brush the tops lightly with the remaining milk, then bake for 10–15 minutes until well risen and golden brown. Best served warm.

COOK'S TIP

Scones are best baked on the day of serving, but you can prepare the mixture in advance: rub the butter into the flour, then stir in the sugar and sultanas and keep in the fridge in a plastic bag or box. When you are ready to make the scones, add the egg and milk and continue as above.

3

Stourhead (WILTSHIRE)

Stourhead was created by a man called Henry Hoare; his father, Richard, had set up Hoare's Bank in 1672 (which is still going strong today) and Henry decided he needed an appropriate country estate. He bought a chunk of Wiltshire countryside in 1717 and set about creating a Palladian villa.

The house was handed down through the Hoare family – Henry, known as 'the Good', gave it to his son, Henry 'the Magnificent'. It carried on through various Hoares until it reached Henry Hugh Arthur. His only son and heir was killed in the First World War, so Henry Hugh decided to hand the estate and all its contents over to the National Trust in 1946.

The house is striking, but Stourhead's USP is undoubtedly the landscape garden. Henry 'the Magnificent' started work on the garden, helped by Henry Flitcroft, a talented architect. The centrepiece of the garden is the lake. As you walk around, you come across a variety of buildings and bridges, giving you the idea of being on a journey – and this was exactly what the Magnificent intended.

One of the buildings is the show-stopping Pantheon. It's like a Wendy-house version of the Pantheon in Rome – well, to be fair, it's a bit bigger than a Wendy house – and is a very accurate miniature representation of the real thing. The grotto is just as impressive. You enter through a little tunnel, and inside it's dark and atmospheric, with the sound of running water and two stirring statues, one of whom is purportedly Tiber, the god of the Roman river.

In fact the walk from the house round the path and back is one of the nicest experiences I've ever had at the National Trust – this despite it raining the whole time!

Cheese Scones

These savoury scones are made with mature cheese and are delicious served warm from the oven with a bowl of soup.

450g self-raising flour	1 egg
115g butter, cubed	150ml milk
140g mature Cheddar cheese, grated	1 tsp English mustard
Salt and freshly ground black pepper	

Preheat the oven to 200°C. Lightly oil a baking sheet.

Sift the flour into a mixing bowl and rub in the butter, using your fingertips, until it resembles fine crumbs. Reserve 25g of the cheese and stir the rest into the flour with a little salt and pepper.

Crack the egg into a jug, add 125ml of the milk and the mustard and whisk together using a fork, then gradually stir into the flour to make a smooth, soft dough.

Turn out the dough onto a lightly floured surface, knead lightly, then cut in half. Shape each half into a ball, flatten slightly and roll out to a circle 15cm in diameter. Cut each circle into quarters and arrange on the baking sheet, leaving space between the quarters so that there is room for them to rise.

Brush the tops lightly with the remaining milk and sprinkle with the reserved cheese. Bake for 12–15 minutes until well risen and golden brown. Best served warm.

Sweet Scones

4
—

Wimpole Estate (Cambridgeshire)

If you made a list of National Trust properties most suited to children, I reckon Wimpole would be in the top five, thanks to the very wonderful farm. There's a piggery (with cute little piglets and sows the size of my car), some cows, Shetland ponies, and even a Shire horse to keep everyone entertained and slightly on edge.

Wimpole Hall is a very large and interesting house, with a chapel, a splendid library, and a plunge pool built in 1792. I was fascinated by the pool – apparently they were quite common at the time, although they were usually located away from the house. The Wimpole Hall we see today has had many different owners from 1640, most of whom seem to have been forced to sell up by mounting debts.

It's frankly astonishing it was still standing in 1936, when Wimpole was let to a Captain George Bambridge and his wife Elsie. She had money – she was the only surviving child of Rudyard Kipling – and so they decided to buy it. George died in 1943, leaving Elsie to spend thirty years doing Wimpole up on her own, before leaving it to the Trust when she died in 1976. It tells you everything that the War Office didn't bother to requisition Wimpole, as it had no electricity or running water.

Elsie sounds like a character. Apparently she hated people coming near the house – she once saw a couple having a picnic in the grounds, so she made a note of their number plate, found where they lived and then went round and had lunch in their garden the following week. It's probably not true, but the fact that it might be says a lot about her!

Ginger and Treacle Scones

Spicy, richly dark scones for an autumn or winter tea.

225g self-raising flour
1 ½ tsp baking powder
2 tsp ground ginger
50g butter, cubed

6 tbsp milk, plus extra to glaze
1 rounded tbsp black treacle

Preheat the oven to 220°C. Grease a baking sheet.

Sift the flour, baking powder and ginger into a mixing bowl and then, using your fingertips, rub in the butter until the mixture resembles fine crumbs.

Warm the milk and treacle together in a small pan until lukewarm. Add to the mixture and mix gently, using a round-bladed knife, to make a soft dough.

Turn out onto a lightly floured surface and knead until smooth, then roll out to about 2cm thick. Stamp out using a 5cm round cutter and place on the baking sheet. Brush the tops with a little milk. Bake just above the centre of the oven for 10–15 minutes until well risen and golden brown.

Transfer to a wire rack to cool slightly. Best served with butter while still slightly warm from the oven.

5

Polesden Lacey (SURREY)

I don't know about you, but I love National Trust properties that have an individual story attached to them, especially when that individual is a bit colourful. Polesden – an attractive estate with breathtaking views of the Surrey Hills – was bought in 1906 by Margaret 'Maggie' Greville and her husband Ronald. It is presented today as she had it in her heyday as an Edwardian society hostess.

Maggie was the 'natural' daughter of William McEwan, the millionaire Scottish brewer. This is a polite way of saying that she was illegitimate, but it turns out that her parents did eventually get married in 1885, when she was twenty-one. I have no idea how society viewed this at the time, because it doesn't sound like the kind of thing that went down particularly well with the Victorians, but it certainly didn't stop her hobnobbing with the great and the good in later life.

Maggie loved her royalty. Visitors to Polesden included Edward VI and George V, and the future George VI and the Queen Mother spent a bit of their honeymoon there. The Queen Mother loved Maggie, describing her as 'so kind and so amusingly unkind' ('skilfully malicious' was another contemporary description of her). If you'd had the pleasure of being entertained by her, chances are that at some point Maggie would have shown you one of her many trinkets and told you how dear, dear Albert had insisted she accept it in gratitude for her marvellous hospitality. A bit of a toady to the last, she apparently left her jewellery and money to various royals, as if they needed it. However, she did leave the estate to the National Trust, so we thank her for that.

Earl Grey Scones

These would be perfect for an elegant afternoon tea.

180ml milk
2–3 Earl Grey teabags
500g self-raising flour
100g caster sugar

125g salted butter, cubed
100g mixed peel
1 egg, beaten
Icing sugar to dust

Warm the milk in a pan or in the microwave to 60°C. Transfer to a jug. Tear open the teabags and stir the tea into the milk. Leave to brew while the milk cools down. (Alternatively leave to brew overnight in the fridge.)

Preheat the oven to 200°C. Line a baking sheet with greaseproof paper.

Sift the flour and sugar into a mixing bowl, add the butter and rub in until it resembles fine crumbs. Add the mixed peel and stir briefly.

Strain in the cooled tea-infused milk, add the egg and mix to form a soft dough. (If too wet, add a little more flour; if too dry, add a touch more milk.)

Turn out onto a lightly floured surface and roll out to about 3cm thick. Stamp out using a 7cm round fluted cutter and transfer to the baking sheet. Gently push the trimmings together, re-roll and stamp out more rounds until you have made ten scones.

Bake for about 15 minutes until golden brown and springy to the touch.

Transfer to a wire rack to cool slightly. Finish with a dusting of icing sugar. Best served warm with butter and marmalade.

6

Hadrian's Wall and Housesteads Fort
(NORTHUMBERLAND)

Hadrian's Wall stretches seventy-three miles from the Tyne to the Solway Firth. It was built in AD 122 – that's almost 1,900 years ago. So if you're feeling a bit old, then it's a great place to remind yourself that you're really not.

Hadrian was Roman emperor between 117 and 138. Rome had expanded into Britain, but Hadrian decided it was time to draw a line signifying where the Empire ended. He ordered the construction of a wall that would stop the 'barbarians' to the north from marauding into Roman territory. The wall was fifteen feet high in places, and eight feet deep. There was a mile-castle (basically a small fort) every mile and a turret every third of a mile, as well as thirteen forts along its length. And it took just six years to build, constructed by Roman legionnaires, the elite soldiers who had the specialist skills required. Once the Romans retreated from Britain, the wall was dismantled over time by people nicking the stones to build castles, houses, even churches.

The National Trust owns a six-mile stretch, from Housesteads Fort (which, like most forts, is shaped like a playing card) to Cawfields, and there's loads to see – you can spend hours just pottering around the remains at Housesteads. Then you might want to wander along to Sycamore Gap, which you might recognise from the scene in *Robin Hood: Prince of Thieves* where Kevin Costner first meets nasty Alan Rickman's men. Or head to Vindolanda, which has an awe-inspiring range of artefacts that were dug from the mud, including the Vindolanda Tablets, an amazing set of letters written by Roman people living in the fort that contain fascinatingly mundane stuff like news of underpants and dinner parties. *Plus ça change*, eh?

Singin' Hinnies

Singin' hinnies are a Northumbrian delicacy. 'Hinnie' is a term of endearment, and the fat makes these flattish scones 'sing' when they are cooking in the traditional way, on a griddle.

225g plain flour
1 tsp baking powder
50g butter, cubed
50g lard, cubed

75g currants
½ tsp salt
4–5 tbsp milk
4–5 tbsp soured cream

Preheat the oven to 200°C and put a baking sheet in the oven. Alternatively, preheat a griddle or a heavy-based frying pan.

Sift the flour and baking powder into a mixing bowl and then, using your fingertips, rub the fats into the flour until the mixture resembles fine crumbs. Add the currants and salt, then add enough of the milk and soured cream to make a soft dough. Knead lightly until smooth.

On a lightly floured surface, roll out to about 1.5cm thick. Stamp out using a 6–7cm round cutter. Transfer to the preheated baking sheet or griddle and cook for 7–8 minutes, then turn and flatten them slightly and cook for 7–8 minutes on the other side until golden. Serve warm with butter – or sprinkle with caster sugar.

COOK'S TIP
Singin' hinny was originally made as one large 'scone', but this recipe makes individual small hinnies.

7

Brownsea Island (Dorset)

Thanks to a 'slow-moving' train, by the time I reached Poole Quay and boarded the boat that takes you across to Brownsea, I had serious doubts that it could possibly be worth the effort. Well, I was wrong. Brownsea Island is one of the most gorgeous places I have ever visited. It's an absolute beaut of an island, with a castle and a church and woodland and lovely views of the sea, plus some fascinating history.

The very first Scout camp was held on Brownsea Island in 1907, when Robert Baden-Powell and twenty boys pitched their tents there. I cannot imagine anything worse than camping, and my career as a Brownie was undistinguished, but I reckon even I would pitch a tent here. It has woodland, beaches, lagoons – everything. A real paradise.

Guglielmo Marconi, the man known for inventing the radio, was a frequent visitor to Brownsea and conducted many of his experiments with wireless telegraphy at the Haven Hotel opposite the island. It's quite strange to think that the man responsible for me having to listen to Magic FM every morning spent so much time in such a tranquil and peaceful place.

There are about 200 red squirrels on the island – sadly I saw not a one of them (October is apparently the best time to spot them). The nearest I came was a fridge magnet in the shop. The John Lewis Partnership leases the castle on Brownsea, renting out five-star accommodation at two-star prices to their staff. Unsurprisingly, there's a four-year waiting list. It would be worth waiting for, though – I can't think of a nicer place to wake up in the morning.

Honey Scones

Enjoy the delicate aroma of honey when these scones come out of the oven.

100g plain wholemeal flour
100g plain white flour
2 tsp baking powder
Pinch of salt
75g butter, cubed

1 tbsp soft light brown sugar
2 tbsp clear honey
50–75ml milk

Preheat the oven to 200°C. Grease a baking sheet.

Sift the flours, baking powder and salt into a mixing bowl and tip in any bran left in the sieve. Using your fingertips, rub in the butter. Add the sugar and mix.

Mix the honey with the milk and stir until the honey has dissolved. Reserve a little for glazing, add the rest to the flour mixture and mix to make a soft dough.

Place the dough on the baking sheet and, using your hands, shape into a flat round about 18cm in diameter. Using a knife, divide the top into eight wedges without cutting all the way through. Bake for 15–20 minutes until pale golden and springy to the touch.

Remove from the oven, brush the top with the reserved honey and milk mixture and return to the oven for a further 5–10 minutes until golden. Serve warm with butter.

Woolsthorpe Manor (LINCOLNSHIRE)

This house is significant not in itself but for its history. It played a big part in the life and work of Sir Isaac Newton, who was born here on Christmas Day in 1642. Isaac's father, who was lord of the manor, died before Isaac was born. His mother then spent a few pregnant months worrying about her future: if she had a boy, he would eventually become lord of the manor and they could both remain at Woolsthorpe. If she had a girl, the two of them would be packed off back to her relatives and the house would pass to someone else. So she was presumably extra-delighted when Isaac popped out.

He was a precocious lad who failed to show the slightest interest in farming, so he was sent off to school, followed by Cambridge University. When the plague struck Cambridge in 1665, Isaac returned to Woolsthorpe and did some of his greatest work at the manor. He spent his *annus mirabilis* producing some of his most important scientific thinking, covering motion, light and gravitation, although he didn't publish his theories until 1687, when *Philosophiæ Naturalis Principia Mathematica* appeared in print. This included his famous theory of gravity.

It's a myth, alas, that he came up with this theory after being hit on the head by an apple. He was a safe distance away when he saw the apple fall from a tree at Woolsthorpe, prompting him to wonder why it dropped straight downwards and not in a random direction. The tree is still there, right outside the house; it fell over in 1816 but re-rooted and continues to grow. It now has offshoots all over the world, ensuring that Newton's legacy lives on at, among other places, MIT in the United States.

Honey, Ginger and Sunflower Scones

With the spicy warmth of ginger and the crunch of sunflower seeds, these scones are perfect with butter – and maybe a little more honey.

500g plain flour
2 tsp baking powder
100g caster sugar
1 tbsp ground ginger
125g butter

25g grated fresh ginger
3 tbsp sunflower seeds
2 tbsp clear honey
1 egg, beaten
Approx. 150ml milk

Preheat the oven to 190°C. Line a baking sheet with greaseproof paper.

Sift the flour, baking powder, sugar and ground ginger into a mixing bowl. Using your fingertips, rub in the butter until the mixture resembles fine crumbs. Stir in the grated ginger and sunflower seeds.

Add the honey, egg and enough milk to make a soft dough.

Turn out onto a floured surface and roll out to about 4cm thick. Stamp out using a 7cm round cutter and place on the baking sheet. Push the trimmings together, knead lightly, re-roll and stamp out more rounds.

Brush the tops lightly with milk and bake for 15–20 minutes or until golden brown.

Giant's Causeway (COUNTRY ANTRIM)

The Giant's Causeway is the only National Trust property that looks like it is made out of scones. (Sadly I am the sole proponent of this particular theory.)

The best-known story behind the Causeway tells how it was built by a giant called Finn McCool. He lived on the Northern Irish coast and decided to build a path over to Scotland so he could do battle against his rival, Benandonner.

As Finn made his way over to Scotland, he spotted Benandonner and realised that he was much bigger than Finn had expected. So he ran home to his wife, Oonagh, and told her of his mistake. She quickly dressed Finn up as a baby and tucked him into their son Oisin's cot, just as Benandonner knocked on the door shouting for Finn to come out and fight.

Oonagh told Benandonner that Finn would be home any minute. When he grew impatient, she offered to introduce him to their baby. Benandonner took one look in the cot and got scared – if the baby was that big, how big was its dad? – and he ran home, ripping up the Causeway behind him so Finn couldn't follow.

There are many other tales – Finn building the Causeway to reach his sweetheart; Finn needing to get home in a hurry and hailing a giant camel (I'm not making this up) – that date back years. There is written evidence of a tourist trade at the Causeway dating from 1700, and tour guides need stories.

But the Causeway itself gives plenty of scope for tall tales. There's a Wishing Chair – a perfect natural throne in the rocks, where you can sit and make a wish (it worked for the Argentinian youth football team apparently, who won the Milk Cup after each player sat in the chair) – the Giant's Boot, the Giant's Fan, and lots more.

Ulster Scones

Bakers' shops in Ulster are full of different shapes and sizes of scones, teabreads and soda breads not seen in the rest of the UK.

250g wholemeal flour
250g strong white flour
½ tsp bicarbonate of soda
75g caster sugar
75g salted butter, cubed

50g chopped glacé cherries or
50g sultanas (optional)
350ml buttermilk
1 egg, beaten
Milk, to brush

Preheat the oven to 220°C. Grease a baking sheet or line it with baking paper.

Sift the two flours together with the bicarbonate of soda and sugar into a mixing bowl and tip in any bran left in the sieve. Using your fingertips, rub in the butter until the mixture resembles fine crumbs. If you are making fruit scones, add the cherries or sultanas and mix them in well.

Stir in the buttermilk and egg and knead lightly to make a soft dough. Do not overwork the dough.

On a lightly floured surface, roll out to about 2.5cm thick and cut the dough into about 24 triangles or rounds, using a 5cm round cutter.

Place on the baking sheet, brush the tops with milk and bake for 10–15 minutes until risen and golden brown.

10

Nostell (West Yorkshire)

Is there any craftsman in history whose name has been more abused than Thomas Chippendale? Born in 1718, he achieved lasting fame as a cabinet-maker, but in the twentieth century it all backfired a bit: in 1943 Walt Disney created two irritating cartoon rodents called Chip 'n' Dale, and then in 1979 along came the Chippendales, a male striptease dance troupe so named because the nightclub where they were formed contained Chippendale-type furniture.

Nostell's mansion was one of twenty-six houses that Chippendale worked on during his career (there are approximately 700 proven pieces of Chippendale furniture in the world and, staggeringly, about 120 of those pieces are to be found here). The original priory was established in the twelfth century and dedicated to St Oswald. The Dissolution of the Monasteries put paid to the priory and the estate passed through the hands of various owners until the Winn family bought it in 1654. The Winns are still going strong – their ancestor, the 4th Baronet St Oswald, gave Nostell to the National Trust in 1953.

Sir Rowland Winn inherited in 1722 and decided to build a new house. This is by and large the massive property we see today, which took a very long time to finish. James Paine spent thirty years working for Sir Rowland, but when his son inherited in 1765 he wanted a different approach and instructed Robert Adam to continue the work. Chippendale was brought in, who as well as furniture provided bed-hangings, curtains, carpets and trimmings. One of the guides observed that Chippendale was the Laurence Llewelyn-Bowen of his day. I'm not sure how Chippendale would feel about that comparison...

Maple and Walnut Scones

Maple and walnut is a classic combination for pastries, cakes and fudge – it's just as good in scones.

500g self-raising flour
125g caster sugar
125g butter, cubed
50g walnut pieces, roughly chopped
 or crushed
150–200ml milk
1 tbsp maple flavouring, essence
 or syrup

TO DECORATE
25g walnut pieces, roughly chopped
 or crushed
100g icing sugar
½ tsp maple flavouring, essence or
 syrup

Preheat the oven to 190°C. Line a baking sheet with baking paper.

Sift the flour and sugar into a mixing bowl and rub in the butter until the mixture resembles fine crumbs. Stir in the walnuts.

Mix the milk and maple flavouring and add just enough liquid to make a soft dough.

Turn out onto a lightly floured surface and roll out to about 3cm thick. Stamp out with a 7cm round cutter and place on the baking sheet. Bake for 20–25 minutes until golden brown and springy to the touch. Transfer to a wire rack to cool (leave the oven on).

Meanwhile, prepare the decoration. Place walnut pieces on a baking sheet and toast in the oven for 5 minutes; leave to cool.

Sift the icing sugar into a bowl. Add the maple flavouring and then add a little cold water, a few drops at a time, and stir until the icing has a dropping consistency. Spoon over the cooled scones and sprinkle the toasted walnuts on top.

33

11

Houghton Mill (CAMBRIDGESHIRE)

I'd wanted to visit Houghton Mill near Huntingdon for ages. When I started my quest, I asked for suggestions on where I could find the best National Trust scones and Houghton got in touch to say 'We do scones. We make them using flour that we mill ourselves.'

What the good people of Houghton should have said is, 'We are a mill that has existed since the 900s. We were once run by a man with the very awesome name of Potto Brown. We nearly got demolished in the 1930s but our local community saved us and gave us to the National Trust. We renovated the place and now every Sunday we start up the mill and we make actual, proper flour that you can actually, properly eat.'

Any 'Bagpuss' fans may be thinking what I was thinking. There is a famous episode when the mice had a chocolate biscuit factory and paraded the chocolate digestives that they were making in front of bemused old Baggers. Except they weren't making anything – it was the same biscuit going round and round. They certainly had me fooled, although in my defence I was only three at the time.

So I had this image of the mill selling bags of supermarket's own brand wholemeal that had been hastily emptied into something more rustic. But no – they really do mill their own flour at Houghton from locally grown wheat, and then they use it to make delicious scones. How awesome is that?

Wholemeal Fruit Scones

When using wholemeal flour in scones, it's important to keep a light touch when kneading and rolling.

490g self-raising flour
70g wholemeal flour
50g caster sugar
140g butter, cubed

50g sultanas
1 egg
200ml milk

Preheat the oven to 190°C. Line a baking sheet with baking paper.

Sift the flours and sugar into a mixing bowl and tip in any bran left in the sieve. Using your fingertips, rub in the butter until the mixture resembles fine crumbs. Gently stir in the sultanas.

Whisk the egg in a jug and add about 150ml of the milk. Add to the flour mixture and, working quickly and lightly using either your fingertips or a round-bladed knife, bring the mixture together to make a soft dough.

Turn out onto a lightly floured surface. Press down gently until the dough is roughly the height of your cutter. At this stage you can use a rolling pin if you want a nice flat top to your scones; if you prefer them more rustic, use your hands to level out the dough to about 3cm thick. Don't press too hard. Stamp out using an 8cm round cutter. Gently push the trimmings together, re-roll and stamp out more rounds.

Place on the baking sheet and brush the tops with milk. Bake for 15–20 minutes or until golden and a knife inserted into the side of a scone comes out clean.

12

—

Hardwick Hall (Derbyshire)

Bess of Hardwick was a major player in Elizabethan society. This extraordinary woman built both Hardwick Hall *and* nearby Chatsworth. She had four husbands, and she and her final hubby were responsible for keeping Mary, Queen of Scots under lock and key for fifteen years before Mary eventually had her head cut off. Bess was also a great friend of Lady Jane Grey before Jane had *her* head cut off.

With getting through four husbands and having a penchant for hanging around with people who got decapitated, you might think Bess was a sort of black-widow type, but it doesn't sound as if she was like that. She loved them all, but was also very canny. Her father had died when she was seven months old and her mother had a terrible time keeping hold of his assets. Bess learned from this, and each marriage left her richer and richer until she was the second wealthiest woman in Britain, after the Queen.

Hardwick Hall was built in 1590, and is ostentatious and stupendous. Bess's initials feature on top of every turret. It was designed by Robert Smythson and contains a number of unusual features for its time: it is symmetrical; the private rooms are on the ground floor, with the public rooms above; and it contains a lot of windows (glass was very expensive at the time), leading to the rhyme, 'Hardwick Hall, more glass than wall'.

It's a large house and many of the rooms are true show-stoppers that make you gape. There are also tapestries that have been in the house since the 1590s – because Chatsworth was the main family residence, Hardwick wasn't modernised as much as it might have been, which is great news for visitors to this wonderful place today.

Rhubarb and Stem Ginger Scones

Bright pink, tender Yorkshire forced rhubarb is available in February and March; after that, use rhubarb from the garden.

750g self-raising flour
½ tsp baking powder
185g caster sugar
185g butter, cubed

200g rhubarb, peeled and cut into
    small dice
1 piece of stem ginger in syrup from
    a jar, cut into very small dice
300ml milk

Preheat the oven to 190°C. Line a baking sheet with greaseproof paper.

Sift the flour, baking powder and sugar into a mixing bowl. Rub in the butter until the mixture resembles fine crumbs. Add the rhubarb and ginger, then about two-thirds of the milk and mix until you have a soft, slightly wet dough, adding a little more milk if needed (it's important not to overmix).

Turn out onto a lightly floured surface and roll out to about 3–4cm thick. Stamp out using an 8cm round cutter and place on the baking sheet. Brush the tops lightly with milk.

Put the scones in the oven and reduce the oven temperature to 180°C. Bake for 20 minutes until risen and golden. Best served warm with clotted cream and jam.

COOK'S TIP

If you want to make these scones outside the rhubarb season, you could use frozen or preserved (bottled or canned) rhubarb. Drain it well and pat dry with paper towel before chopping. You may find you need to use very little milk.

13

—

Scotney Castle (KENT)

Scotney is a fantastic place. It has two main parts: the 'new' house completed in 1843 and the old castle, which dates back to medieval times.

The old part was originally built by Roger Ashburnham in c1378–80. The Darell family came along after that. They owned Scotney for 350 years, during which time they knocked down bits of the Old Castle and rebuilt the place to suit their needs. Their needs included a priest hole, as they were Catholics and they needed somewhere to hide Father Blount during tricky times.

The house was then bought by Edward Hussey in 1778. He lived in the Old Castle until he committed suicide. His grandson, Edward Hussey III, decided to build a mock Elizabethan home and leave the old place as a picturesque ruin.

And that's what I loved about Scotney – it's a real contrast of styles. You can go from medieval to real Elizabethan to faux Elizabethan to the 1950s in ten minutes. And the house has a lived-in homely feel – Betty Hussey, wife of Edward's great-nephew Christopher, died just a few years ago but she asked that the cat was allowed to remain and so its food bowls are sitting in the kitchen as if Betty had just popped out.

National Trust guidebooks always contain at least one WOWZERS! factoid and Scotney's one is that Betty did the kitchen up with the proceeds from the place being used in the Richard Gere film *Yanks*. Richard Gere at Scotney Castle. Who knew?

Salted Caramel and Apple Scones

Rich and luxurious scones for an indulgent afternoon tea.

500g self-raising flour	SALTED CARAMEL SAUCE
100g caster sugar	25g butter
125g butter, cubed	35g soft light brown sugar
300g cooking apples	100ml double cream
4 tbsp milk	Good pinch of sea salt

Preheat the oven to 190°C. Line a baking sheet with baking paper.

To make the caramel sauce: put the butter, sugar and cream in a pan over a low heat, stirring occasionally until the mixture thickens. Add the salt and leave to cool.

To make the scones: sift the flour and sugar into a mixing bowl. Using your fingertips, rub in the butter until the mixture resembles fine crumbs.

Peel, core and finely chop the apples. Add the apples and caramel sauce to the scone mix – reserving a small amount of the sauce to glaze the scones. Add the milk and mix to make a firm dough.

Turn out onto a floured surface and roll out to about 3cm thick. Stamp out using a 7cm round cutter. Place on the baking sheet and bake for about 20 minutes until springy to the touch. Transfer to a wire rack and leave to cool completely.

Once the scones are cool, glaze with the reserved caramel sauce.

14

Speke Hall (LIVERPOOL)

A lot of National Trust properties have a nice little stream or a pond somewhere on the estate. Speke Hall has the River Mersey. I knew it was there, but still did a double take when I saw it. As you walk through the entrance, there it is: that massive river, with the industrial trappings of Ellesmere Port on the other side.

Speke Hall is a rare Tudor timber-framed house that was mostly built in the 1500s, although bits of it date back further. It was only ever owned by two families, the Norrises and the Watts – William Norris built the Great Hall and Great Parlour. Edward Norris inherited in 1568; he was reported for harbouring a Catholic priest and it is believed that the priest hole dates from then; you can just see the ladder behind the panelling in the Green Bedroom.

In 1795 the Norrises sold up to Richard Watt, a man who had profited greatly from slave labour in his plantations. Speke Hall was in a sorry state by this stage, but was slowly renovated through the nineteenth century. It was finally inherited by young Adelaide Watt, whose father died aged thirty, and once of age herself, she ran Speke until her death in 1921.

Adelaide had no children and wanted a descendant of the Norris family to take on the house after her death. However, an airfield had opened next to the Hall at the start of the twentieth century – it is now Liverpool John Lennon Airport – and Adelaide guessed other developments might put off future residents. So she made the proviso that if the Norrises didn't want to move in, then Speke Hall would be given to the National Trust. And that's exactly what happened.

Wet Nelly Scones

The unusual name of these scones comes from their main
ingredient, Wet Nelly, a spicy moist bread pudding from Liverpool.

450g self-raising flour

3 tsp baking powder

125g butter, cubed

50g caster sugar

1 egg

Approx. 400g Wet Nelly (see page 42),
cold, crumbled

Approx. 120–150ml milk

Preheat the oven to 200°C and grease a baking sheet.

Sift the flour and baking powder into a mixing bowl. Add the butter
and rub in using your fingertips until it resembles fine crumbs. Stir in
the sugar.

Add the egg, the Wet Nelly and about 100ml of the milk and mix.
Gradually add more milk until you have a soft dough.

On a floured surface, roll out the dough to about 3cm thick. Stamp
out using a 7cm round cutter and place on the baking sheet. Brush the
tops lightly with milk.

Bake for 15–20 minutes or until golden brown and a knife inserted
into the side of a scone comes out clean. Transfer to a wire rack to
cool slightly before serving.

COOK'S TIP
Make the Wet Nelly a day or two before you want
to make these scones – or cheat and buy ready-made
bread pudding.

Wet Nelly

Wet Nelly is a Liverpool name for bread pudding – if you don't use it in your scones, it's delicious served warm with custard.

---

1 small loaf (approx. 300g) of stale
   brown bread, crusts cut off, cut
   into large cubes
375g mixed dried fruit
75g butter

650ml milk, warmed
100g soft dark brown sugar
1½ tsp mixed spice
3 eggs

Put the bread and fruit in a large mixing bowl. Mix the butter with the milk and pour over the bread and fruit. Leave to soak for at least 4 hours, or (preferably) overnight.

Preheat the oven to 160°C and grease a deep 18cm square cake tin.

Add the sugar, spice and eggs to the soaked mixture and mix well. Pour into the prepared tin and bake for 1¼–1½ hours until springy to the touch.

Leave to firm up for 15–20 minutes before serving hot, or leave to cool and cut into squares.

COOK'S TIP
Save half the Wet Nelly if you want to use it to make scones (see previous page).

What is Wet Nelly?

Wet Nelly is a moist version of a fruit cake known as Nelson cake.

It was originally made from broken biscuits and pastry remnants; dried fruit was added and the mixture was soaked in syrup.

You could include some broken biscuits, brioche, leftover sponge or fruit cake, in place of some of the bread.

Chocolate Scones

15

Ickworth (SUFFOLK)

Ickworth is breathtaking. The house is formed of a rotunda with two enormous wings curving round either side. It looks like an art gallery – and that's exactly what its builder intended for it. Frederick Hervey, who was known as the Earl-Bishop because he was both an earl (of Bristol) and a bishop of Derry, wanted it to be a showcase for his art collection, which unfortunately was confiscated by Napoleon before he could get it back to England. The whole place is quite dramatic, with huge rooms, and the East Wing is now the posh Ickworth Hotel.

What really sets the pulse racing at Ickworth is its salacious history. The Herveys took ownership of Ickworth in the mid-fifteenth century. They were very influential at court, but they were also total scandal magnets.

Taking a brief sample chronologically: John, Lord Hervey, the son of the first Earl and his second wife, shared a mistress with the Prince of Wales, and had a 10-year relationship with another man although he never separated from his wife, Molly Lepel.

The Third Earl of Bristol, Augustus Hervey – Lord Hervey and Molly's son – was known as the English Casanova. His conquests included princesses, duchesses, actresses, singers, dancers and even nuns. He secretly married one Elizabeth Chudleigh, who then went on to enjoy a bigamous marriage with the Duke of Kingston, causing public outrage.

Elizabeth Hervey Foster Cavendish, the daughter of the Earl-Bishop who built Ickworth, enjoyed a *ménage-à-trois* with the Duke and Duchess of Devonshire for 25 years, eventually marrying the Duke following the Duchess' death in 1806.

As the glory days of the country house came to an end in the post-war period, the Hervey's tenure at Ickworth changed but not without further scandal.

Chocolate and Marshmallow Scones

Enjoy these scones with a mug of hot chocolate; a perfect way to warm up after a winter walk.

500g self-raising flour
40g cocoa powder
1 tsp baking powder
55g soft brown sugar
100g salted butter, cubed

70g milk chocolate drops
55g mini marshmallows
1 egg, beaten
Approx. 200ml milk

Preheat the oven to 190°C. Line a baking sheet with greaseproof paper.

Sift the flour, cocoa, baking powder and sugar into a mixing bowl, add the butter and rub in until it resembles fine crumbs. Add the chocolate drops and marshmallows and mix to distribute them evenly.

Add the egg and then gradually pour in the milk; add just enough milk to make a damp dough – it should not be wet or sloppy.

Turn out onto a lightly floured surface and roll out to about 3cm thick. Stamp out using a 7cm round fluted cutter and place on the baking sheet. Gently knead the trimmings together, re-roll and stamp out more rounds.

Bake for 18–20 minutes until risen and springy to the touch. Transfer to a wire rack to cool slightly. Best served warm with chocolate spread.

COOK'S TIP
You can put a few marshmallows on top of the scones for the last few minutes of baking so they go gooey on the inside.

16

Acorn Bank (Cumbria)

I very rarely join tours at National Trust properties, but the tour guide at Acorn Bank, near Penrith, was excellent. The estate, which boasts a restored working water mill, was once owned by the Knights Templar, who used it as a safe haven for travellers in the thirteenth century. In 1543, it was acquired by the local Dalston family and it remained with their descendants until the 1930s, when the estate was acquired by Dorothy Una Ratcliffe and her husband Capt. Noel McGrigor Phillips. She gave it to the National Trust in 1950 – they supported her efforts to stop a munitions dump near the estate and she gratefully promised the house to them.

Dorothy sounds like a real character – when James Lees-Milne went to negotiate the terms of her leaving the house to the Trust, he accidentally left his notes behind. Dorothy read them and found all the uncomplimentary things he had said about them (in his diary, he described her husband as 'a grubby, red-visaged, hirsute old teddy bear'). She took offence and, although she left the Trust the house as planned, she took everything out of it – hence the lack of furniture in it today.

The woman on reception told me excitedly that there were some newts in the pond. I am no wildlife expert and thought I wouldn't recognise a newt if it fell on me. But I wandered around for a look and I was amazed – there were loads of them. And after my visit to Acorn Bank I finally understand the point of putting fairy houses in trees; when I found the little green door and jetty, complete with miniature boat, I realised that children walking round here must go absolutely nuts with excitement. I was quite excited and I'm in my forties.

Chocolate and Hazelnut Scones

Studded with chocolate and nuts, these scones are sweet enough to eat on their own – or try them with whipped cream.

500g self-raising flour
100g caster sugar
125g butter, cubed
75g chocolate chips, or chocolate bar
   cut into small chunks
50g hazelnuts, chopped
225ml milk

TO DECORATE
15g hazelnuts, chopped
50g icing sugar
½ tbsp cocoa

Preheat the oven to 190°C. Line a baking sheet with baking paper.

Sift the flour and sugar into a mixing bowl and then, using your fingertips, rub in the butter until the mixture resembles fine crumbs. Add the chocolate chips and hazelnuts and mix until combined.

Add the milk and mix to make a soft dough.

Turn out onto a floured surface and roll out to about 3cm thick. Stamp out using a 7cm round cutter and place on the baking sheet.

Bake for 20–25 minutes until risen and golden brown. Transfer to a wire rack to cool (leave the oven on).

Next, prepare the decoration. Place the hazelnuts on a baking sheet and put in the oven for 5 minutes, then leave to cool.

To make the chocolate icing, sift the icing sugar and cocoa into a bowl. Add a little cold water, a few drops at a time, and stir until the icing has a dropping consistency. Once the scones are cool, drizzle or pipe the icing on top and then sprinkle the toasted hazelnuts over.

17

Goddards House & Gardens (NORTH YORKSHIRE)

I would move into the house at Goddards tomorrow if the National Trust would let me. It was built in the 1920s by a Yorkshire architect called Walter Brierley and it feels like a real family home. What's even lovelier is that you're allowed to sit on the chairs and play games in the playroom and basically pretend you live there. There is even something I've never encountered before at a Trust property (or anywhere else for that matter) – an honesty box for sherry! You just pop your two pounds in and help yourself to a glass.

Goddards was the home of Noel Goddard Terry, creator of that most genius of products, Terry's Chocolate Orange. It all began when Robert Berry opened a sweet shop in 1767; his niece married a chemist called Joseph Terry, who joined Robert's business and eventually took it over and renamed it Terry's of York. It was then that they started to produce chocolate – previously it had been boiled sweets all the way.

You can just about see the old chocolate factory from the picturesque garden. It was closed down in 2005 when Kraft, who took over Terry's in the early 1990s, moved production overseas (the Chocolate Orange is now made in Poland and Terry's All Gold in Belgium). And the garden provides more opportunities to lounge about and imagine you live there, with tables and chairs scattered all around. While you do, why not picture yourself indulging in the Chocolate Orange's unlikely predecessor – the Chocolate Apple? I was astounded to learn during my visit that such a delicacy was once produced. Perhaps they should bring it back . . .

Chocolate Orange Scones

A quirky twist on a confectionery classic.

500g self-raising flour
90g caster sugar
125g butter, cubed
½ Terry's Chocolate Orange, broken
    into chunks

Grated zest of 1 orange
1 egg
180ml milk

Preheat the oven to 190°C. Line a baking sheet with baking paper.

Sift the flour and sugar into a mixing bowl and rub in the butter until it resembles fine crumbs. Add the Chocolate Orange and stir through the mixture, along with the orange zest.

Beat the egg with the milk and gradually pour about three-quarters of this liquid into the flour mixture to form a soft dough; add more liquid if necessary.

Turn out onto a floured surface and roll out to 3cm thick. Stamp out using a 7cm round cutter, place on the baking sheet and brush the tops with the milk and egg mixture.

Bake for about 15 minutes until risen and golden brown.

Transfer to a wire rack to cool slightly. Best served warm with butter and orange marmalade.

18

Finch Foundry (Devon)

The first thing I should probably tell you about Finch Foundry is that it isn't a foundry, it's a forge. I had no clue what the difference was before my visit to Finch, but now I know: a foundry pours molten metal into moulds to create products; a forge heats metal so the items can be hammered into shape.

Although Finch Foundry operated from 1814, there had been water-powered mills in the area for over 700 years. In 1814, when the Devon woollen industry collapsed, the mill here became a forge under the management of the Finch family. They produced a huge range of edge-tools – do you know what a Cornish furze hook likes like, or a Devon potato chopper? Anyway, the Finch family also made wheel parts, coffin boards, mallets . . . it's incredible to think that they produced 400 tools *a day* at their peak. Finch Foundry kept going until 1960, when part of the building collapsed.

Of course, all those tools had to be sold as well as made. In 1822, no cart was available to take Susannah Finch, wife of William, to Tavistock Fair, so she walked the twenty miles with a quantity of bill-hooks, despite being heavily pregnant. When she returned, she had sold all of the bill-hooks and given birth to a baby girl.

Strangely, the heat from the foundry was used in the nineteenth century to dry bedraggled children! They would sometimes get soaked walking the three miles to school, so the enterprising headteacher would occasionally send them along to Finch Foundry with a note saying, 'Dear Mr Finch, please dry out these children.'

Triple Chocolate Scones

Chocolate is in season all year round, but these scones are a special treat at Easter time.

500g self-raising flour
70g cocoa powder
1 heaped tsp baking powder
70g soft light brown sugar
140g butter, cubed
115g white chocolate drops

115g milk chocolate drops
2 eggs, beaten
1 tsp vanilla essence
Approx. 200ml milk

Preheat the oven to 190°C. Line a large baking sheet with baking paper.

Sift the flour, cocoa, baking powder and sugar into a mixing bowl. Add the butter and rub in until it resembles fine crumbs. Add 75g of the white chocolate drops and 75g of the milk chocolate drops and mix briefly to distribute them evenly.

Make a well in the centre of the mixture, add the eggs and vanilla essence and then gradually pour in the milk; add just enough milk to make a damp dough – it should not be wet or sloppy.

Turn out onto a lightly floured surface and roll out to about 4cm thick. Stamp out using an 8cm round fluted cutter and place on the baking sheet. Gently knead the trimmings together, re-roll and stamp out more rounds. Brush the tops with milk.

Bake for 16–18 minutes until springy to the touch. Transfer to a wire rack to cool.

Melt the remaining white and milk chocolate drops and drizzle over the scones.

19

Bodiam Castle (SUSSEX)

I love a good castle, especially one that looks like it's been drawn by a six-year-old, and Bodiam Castle near Tunbridge Wells is a corker. Even the most unimaginative, Playstation-obsessed kid in the world couldn't fail to be inspired by it.

The castle itself is incredible. I think it's the moat that does it – you walk across a little bridge and into the ruined castle, and with a bit of imagination you picture what it must have been like in the fourteenth century. But from outside you can really see how formidable it must have looked. Sir Edward Dalyngrigge was given permission to build it in 1385, when Richard II gave him 'licence to crenellate'. If you look up at the battlements and see the bits cut out like missing teeth (where they fired arrows and poured boiling tar from), they are the crenels. By 'crenellating' his home, Edward was building a fortress that could help defend the realm. Some cynics question Dalyngrigge's motives and suggest that defensively Bodiam wasn't all that special; what he really wanted to do was make people think *he* was a bit special.

Whatever the truth of that, it's still a charming castle in a terrific location. Inside there are plenty of exhibits, such as a man making arrows and another making armour. The armourer was moaning about his bellows not working properly – I couldn't work out if it was part of the performance or not. They had archery and cannons and a really brilliant display of a trebuchet – a woman explained how it worked and then fired it into the moat ('We just need to wait for the ducks to get out of the way,' she said, matter-of-factly).

Raspberry and White Chocolate Scones

Tangy raspberries are complemented by rich white chocolate. Alternatively, try swapping the raspberries for grated orange zest.

500g self-raising flour
125g caster sugar
125g salted butter, cubed
125g fresh raspberries

125g white chocolate drops
2 eggs, beaten
150–180ml milk
Icing sugar to dust

Preheat the oven to 190°C. Line a baking sheet with greaseproof paper.

Sift the flour and sugar into a mixing bowl, add the butter and rub in until it resembles fine crumbs. Add the raspberries and chocolate drops and mix briefly to distribute them evenly.

Make a well in the centre of the mixture, add the eggs and then gradually pour in the milk; add just enough milk to make a damp dough – it should not be wet or sloppy.

Turn out onto a lightly floured surface and roll out to about 4cm thick. Stamp out using an 8cm round fluted cutter and place on the baking sheet. Gently knead the trimmings together, re-roll and stamp out more rounds.

Bake for 18–20 minutes or until springy to the touch. Transfer to a wire rack to cool.

Before serving, dust with icing sugar. Alternatively, melt some extra white chocolate to drizzle over the top.

Savoury
Scones

20

Waddesdon Manor (BUCKINGHAMSHIRE)

Some National Trust properties are very understated: an old mill; a crumbling tower; a piece of moorland. And then there are some properties that come into view doing high kicks and going, 'Yoohoo! Here I am! A French Renaissance-style château built by the Rothschilds!' Waddesdon Manor belongs in the latter category, not least because it *is* a French Renaissance-style château built by the Rothschilds.

It's almost like a tornado ripped through the Loire Valley, picked up a château and then deposited it just off the M40. It was built in the 1870s. Baron Ferdinand de Rothschild, a member of the distinguished banking family and later a Member of Parliament, bought the land from the Duke of Marlborough and commissioned a French architect, Gabriel-Hippolyte Destailleur, to create a brand-new building in the style of the French châteaux he admired so much.

Ferdinand seems to have used Waddesdon chiefly for two things: 1) housing his collection of art, furniture, china, clocks and mechanical elephant (apparently it flaps its ears and trunk when wound up), you name it; and 2) entertaining kings, queens, politicians, archbishops, etc and showing off said collections.

The rooms are exquisite, and each one is a treasure trove of charming items. Because Waddesdon was left by Ferdinand to his fastidious sister Alice, and then passed to their nephew, James, before being handed over to the National Trust, much of the house and contents are just as Ferdinand had them.

Blue Cheese and
Hazelnut Scones

This method is for regular scones, but for a party you could make a larger number of smaller scones (reduce the cooking time slightly).

300g plain flour
300g self-raising flour
2 tsp baking powder
1 tbsp caster sugar
Pinch of salt
160g unsalted butter, cubed

120g mild Stilton, crumbled
85g hazelnuts, roasted, then finely
 chopped
200–300ml milk
1 egg, beaten (optional)

Preheat the oven to 190°C. Line a baking sheet with greaseproof paper.

Sift the flours, baking powder, sugar and salt into a mixing bowl. Add the butter and rub in using your fingertips until it resembles fine crumbs. Add the cheese and nuts and mix until evenly distributed.

Add 200ml of the milk and mix until the dough starts to come together. Gradually add more milk, adding just enough to make a slightly sticky dough.

Turn out onto a lightly floured surface and roll out to about 3cm thick. Stamp out using a 7cm round cutter and place on the baking sheet. Brush the tops lightly with milk or beaten egg.

Bake for 15–20 minutes or until risen and golden brown.

Transfer to a wire rack to cool slightly. Serve warm with butter and pear or apple jam.

21

Baddesley Clinton (WARWICKSHIRE)

Baddesley Clinton, a lovely moated manor house, is one of many Catholic houses to be fitted with a priest hole by Nicholas Owen during the time of Elizabeth I and James I. Nick was arrested and tortured in 1594 and again in 1606, when he died as a result; he was canonised in 1970.

You can still see the priest holes at Baddesley Clinton. I loved the way the guide said, 'There are three *that we know of,*' as if Nicholas was so cunning that some of his hidey holes are still hiding today. But Baddesley Clinton's history began before the Reformation. Here's a quick run-down of three of its most famous inhabitants.

John Brome – murdered! In 1438, the house was bought by a lawyer called John Brome. He was murdered in a church porch in London by John Herthill during a quarrel over property.

Nicholas Brome – double murderer! John's son, Nicholas, avenged his dad and murdered Herthill in 1471. Then one day he found the local priest flirting with Mrs Brome, so he murdered him. To make up for his crimes, Nicholas built the tower at the nearby church. Fair enough.

Henry Ferrers – friend of Catholics! Not a hanging offence today, but when, in 1590, Henry leased Baddesley out to the Vaux sisters, two fervent Catholics who used the place to harbour Jesuit priests, he was committing treason. And the punishment for treason was to be hanged, drawn and quartered, which was not very pleasant. Not only that, Henry also leased a place in London to Thomas Percy, one of the Gunpowder crew, who actually stored the gang's gunpowder there. Perhaps Henry had friends in high places to have got away with this, but he did, dying in 1633 aged eighty-four.

Ploughman's Scones

Great served with cream cheese and a favourite chutney.

450g self-raising flour
2 tsp baking powder
1 tbsp caster sugar
115g butter, cubed
230g mature Cheddar cheese, grated
1 apple, peeled and diced

4 or 5 pickled onions, roughly
    chopped
Pinch of salt and freshly ground
    black pepper
1 egg, beaten
Approx. 200ml milk

Preheat the oven to 190°C. Line a baking sheet with greaseproof paper.

Sift the flour, baking powder and sugar into a mixing bowl. Add the butter and rub in using your fingertips until the mixture resembles fine crumbs.

Stir in most of the cheese (reserving a little to top the scones), the apple, pickled onions, salt and pepper, then add the egg and enough milk to make a soft dough.

Turn out onto a lightly floured surface and roll out to about 4cm thick. Stamp out using a 7cm round cutter. Knead the trimmings together lightly, re-roll and stamp out more rounds. Place on the baking sheet. Brush the tops with milk and sprinkle with a little grated cheese.

Bake for 15–20 minutes until golden brown.

COOK'S TIP
If you like, you can add some chopped ham
to the mix along with the apple.

22

—

Penrhyn Castle (Gwynedd)

What would you do if you received a call one day saying that Richard Branson had died, leaving everything to you in his will? All of his businesses and a huge sprawling estate with a house on it? The only drawback being that the estate is in North Wales and you live miles away and have never even visited the area?

This is sort of what happened to a man called George Hay Dawkins in 1808. His distant cousin Richard Pennant was the owner of sugar plantations in Jamaica as well as slate quarries in Wales. When he died childless, he left George everything.

I don't know what you would do – I don't even know what I would do – but George decided to spend twenty years and an estimated £100 million in today's money building a 'fairy castle'.

Yes, this ancient-looking fortress might look a thousand years old but it was actually built less than 200 years ago. George didn't want to build a Georgian house. With its location high on a hill near to Caernarfon Castle and Conwy Castle and its views to the mountains of Snowdonia and the Menai Strait, he wanted something spectacular. Twenty years and a king's ransom later, he got it.

But if you think the exterior is impressive, you should see the inside. It is quite literally *stupendous* and probably the most amazing interior I have ever seen at the Trust.

But it is very sobering to look at Penrhyn knowing that it was built on the profits of slavery – our friend George opposed the electoral reform that led to the emancipation of slaves in 1833, and he was paid almost £15,000 for the 764 slaves that were freed from his estates.

Welsh Cheese and Herb Scones

With their warm herby aroma and plenty of tasty cheese, these are a satisfying addition to high tea.

450g self-raising flour
2 tsp baking powder
1 tsp salt
100g butter, cubed
1 tsp mixed dried herbs

225g mature Cheddar or other strong
  cheese, grated
120ml milk
120ml water

Preheat the oven to 220°C. Grease a baking sheet.

Sift the flour, baking powder and salt into a mixing bowl. Add the butter and rub in using your fingertips until the mixture resembles fine crumbs. Add the herbs and 175g of the cheese and stir to mix.

Add the milk and water and mix to make a soft dough.

Turn out onto a floured surface and roll out to about 2.5cm thick. Stamp out using a 6cm round cutter. Place on the baking sheet and top each scone with a little of the remaining grated cheese.

Bake for 10 minutes until golden. Transfer to a wire rack to cool slightly. Serve warm or cold with butter.

23

Souter Lighthouse (Tyne and Wear)

I often wonder what happened to my science teacher, Mr Goodwin. He did his best, poor man, but I must have driven him mad. To this day, I remain totally and shamefully clueless about all things scientific, electricity being the biggest mystery of all. My brain just isn't wired that way.

So I was a bit worried that I wouldn't like Souter Lighthouse in South Shields, about three miles south of the River Tyne. Built in 1871 by those science-loving Victorians, it was the first lighthouse in the world to be powered by AC electricity. I was concerned that there would be loads of machinery and people talking about watts, and my mind would start to wander. But they have fantastic volunteers at Souter who explain everything, from the workings of the apparatus through to the day-to-day lives of the lighthouse keepers who looked after the place, from its opening through to its closure in 1988. I must admit that some of the technicalities went over my head, but Souter has much to recommend it.

It's very pretty: with its red and white hoops it's like a picture postcard of a lighthouse. It has a foghorn, which they still sound on Sundays, and you can see an example of a cottage where the lighthouse keepers lived. It was an incredibly important addition to safety on what was the most hazardous stretch of coastline in the country; in 1860 alone there were twenty shipwrecks in the surrounding area. Watch out, though – the lighthouse is reportedly haunted by the ghost of a former keeper!

Leek and Onion Scones

This recipe comes from Northumberland, which borders Tyne & Wear, where a leek scone is served with a steaming bowl of soup, or with cheese, in place of bread or biscuits.

1 tbsp olive oil
1 large leek, cleaned and finely chopped (you can use the whole leek)
1 small onion, finely chopped
Pinch of caster sugar

450g self-raising flour
2 tsp baking powder
Pinch of salt
115g butter, cubed
250ml milk

Preheat the oven to 220°C. Grease a baking sheet or line it with baking paper.

Heat the oil in a pan and sauté the leek and onion with the pinch of sugar until soft.

Sift the flour, baking powder and salt into a mixing bowl. Add the butter and rub in using your fingertips until the mixture resembles fine crumbs. Stir in the leek and onion mixture and enough milk to make a soft dough.

Turn out onto a floured surface and knead lightly. Roll out to about 2.5cm thick. Stamp out using a 7cm round cutter. Knead the trimmings together lightly, re-roll and stamp out more rounds. Place on the baking sheet and brush the tops with milk.

Bake for about 12–15 minutes or until golden brown.

24

Sudbury Hall (DERBYSHIRE)

The Norman Conquest has a lot to answer for. Among the many Normans who came to Britain in 1066 was a William de Vernon, who was given some land as a thank you. He spawned many generations of Vernons, who broke off into different branches – one set built Hanbury Hall (see p.110), while another offshoot inherited the Sudbury estate in Derbyshire.

Henry Vernon, who inherited Sudbury, died in 1569, leaving his property to his two sons – John inherited Sudbury, while Henry got an estate in Staffordshire. The brothers appear to have been thick as thieves, until Henry married a woman called Dorothy.

For some reason, John did not approve of Dorothy, and when Henry died in 1592 he wanted to stop her getting her hands on all of the family estates. So he married a woman called Mary, the widow of his cousin, who handily already had a son called Edward Vernon.

John died in 1600 without an heir of this own, and so Dorothy and Mary went into battle for the property. It was eventually sorted out in time-honoured fashion: Mary's son, Edward, and Dorothy's daughter, Margaret, were married off to each other – it's not known what they thought of this – and they were given a house at Sudbury.

We can probably assume that Edward and Margaret did find something in common, because the Sudbury Hall we see today was built by their grandson, George, after he inherited in 1660. Interestingly, George's mother was also a Vernon from another branch of the family AND he himself married a Catherine Vernon after his first two wives died.

The Vernons have remained at Sudbury ever since – it was let out for three years from 1839 to Queen Adelaide, widow of William IV – but in 1967 the 10th Lord Vernon offered the estate to the National Trust. He built himself a house on the estate that is still owned by Vernons today.

Stilton and Cranberry Scones

These scones have a Christmassy feel, but they're just as good at other times of year.

450g self-raising flour
2 tsp baking powder
1 tbsp caster sugar
115g butter, cubed
115g Stilton cheese, crumbled
115g Cheddar cheese, grated

115g fresh or dried cranberries
1 egg, beaten
Approx. 200ml milk

Preheat the oven to 190°C. Line a baking sheet with greaseproof paper.

Sift the flour, baking powder and sugar into a mixing bowl. Add the butter and rub in using your fingertips until the mixture resembles fine crumbs.

Stir in the Stilton, Cheddar and cranberries, then add the egg and enough milk to make a soft dough.

Turn out onto a floured surface and roll out to about 4cm thick. Stamp out using a 7cm round cutter. Knead the trimmings together lightly, re-roll and stamp out more rounds. Place on the baking sheet and brush the tops with milk.

Bake for 15–20 minutes until golden brown.

25

Packwood House (WARWICKSHIRE)

Packwood House was originally built in around 1570 by William Fetherstone. The Fetherstones and their descendants continued to own the house until 1869, when it was sold to a solicitor. The Ash family, who had made their fortune in zinc, bought it at auction in 1904, and Packwood was given to the National Trust in 1941 by Graham Baron Ash. He preferred to use his middle name, so everyone called him Baron Ash, even though he was no more an actual baron than I am. A rogue comma was also inserted on one occasion, so it became Graham, Baron Ash. This is ingenious. If Mr Sugar had called his son Lord instead of Alan, he could have saved him the bother of flogging all those computers.

Baron Ash gave the house to the National Trust on the condition that it must be kept exactly as he had it, right down to the position of the furniture. After he handed Packwood over, he went to live in a castle in Suffolk; although he remained friendly with the Packwood gardener, he didn't agree with how it was being run and when he died in 1980 he left none of his £3 million estate to the Trust. (His niece, however, gave them a generous bequest that enabled the purchase of nearby Baddesley Clinton.)

There is a famous Yew Garden at Packwood, which dates back to the mid-nineteenth century and is supposed the represent the Sermon on the Mount, with sixteen of the great yews being known as the 'Evangelists' and the 'Apostles' and a single yew at the summit called 'the Master'. Sadly, and unforgivably, having failed to read up on Packwood before my visit, I only found out about the yew garden *after* my visit.

Cheese, Spring Onion and Bacon Breakfast Scones

Hearty scones for breakfast or lunch. At Packwood they pick the spring onions for this recipe straight from their kitchen garden.

500g self-raising flour
125g butter, cubed
90g mature Cheddar cheese, grated
90g bacon, cooked and finely
  shredded

2 spring onions, finely chopped
Salt and freshly ground black pepper
1 egg
Approx. 180ml milk

Preheat the oven to 190°C. Line a large baking sheet with greaseproof paper.

Sift the flour into a mixing bowl, add the butter and rub in until it resembles fine crumbs. Add most of the cheese (reserving a little to top the scones), the bacon and spring onions, salt and pepper and mix until evenly combined.

Mix the egg with three-quarters of the milk. Gradually add the liquid to the bowl until the mixture comes together and forms a soft dough.

Turn the dough out onto a floured surface and cut in half. Roll each half into a ball and flatten slightly, then place on the baking sheet and slice into five wedges. Sprinkle with the reserved cheese.

Bake for about 15 minutes until risen and golden brown.

26

Attingham (SHROPSHIRE)

There's nothing I like more than a really amazing National Trust factette. The kind of have-to-read-it-five-times-just-to-be-sure-you-read-it-right factette. At Attingham, I discovered one such factette: Thomas, 2nd Lord Berwick, was the owner of a working model of Vesuvius. I have to say, if I made a list of all the things in the world I wanted, a working model of Vesuvius would be 28,237th, just after Megadeth concert tickets and a harpoon.

That's not the only fascinating thing I discovered at Attingham. It was built by Noel Hill, 1st Lord Berwick, in 1782–5. It was inherited by his son Thomas – the one with the volcano – in 1789, who at the age of forty-one married a seventeen-year-old courtesan and then went on a crazy spending spree that bankrupted them. Attingham eventually passed to his brother Richard, who apparently 'swallowed more wine than any man in the county' and died in 1848 after six years in charge.

Fortunately his sensible son, another Richard, inherited and put the estate back on an even keel. He did this by modernising the way that the farms on the estate were run, introducing new agricultural techniques.

Sadly, the next two owners of Attingham showed less interest in the estate, and it was tenanted and unloved by the time that Thomas, 8th Lord Berwick, inherited in 1947. With his wife, Teresa, he began a project to restore the place, working to a very limited budget. He then gifted it to National Trust, ensuring the preservation of this fine Georgian country house.

Shropshire Blue
and Fig Scones

Shropshire Blue cheese has an orange colour, from annatto, a natural colouring; if you can't find Shropshire Blue, Stilton has a similarly tangy flavour.

500g self-raising flour
2 tsp baking powder
125g butter, cubed
60g Shropshire Blue cheese, crumbled

120g Cheddar cheese, grated
2 dried figs, chopped
Approx. 150ml milk

Preheat the oven to 190°C. Line a baking sheet with greaseproof paper.

Sift the flour and baking powder into a mixing bowl and, using your fingertips, rub in the butter until the mixture resembles fine crumbs. Add the Shropshire Blue, 60g of the Cheddar and the figs and stir to combine.

Add enough milk to make a soft dough.

Turn out onto a floured surface and roll out to about 3cm thick. Stamp out using a 7cm round cutter. Place on the baking sheet and sprinkle with a little grated Cheddar.

Bake for 12–18 minutes until risen and golden brown.

27

A la Ronde (DEVON)

I've always been an enormous fan of souvenir tat, filling my cupboards
with bits and pieces from all over the world, but two cousins called
Jane and Mary Parminter make me look like an amateur. In the 1790s
they built a whole house, A la Ronde, near Exmouth, to store their
souvenirs of the Grand Tour.

This ingenious house has sixteen sides, allowing the sun to shine into
different rooms at different times of the day. At the centre of the house
is the Octagon, a room where the cousins could entertain their guests.
A la Ronde is famous for its Shell Gallery at the top of the house.
It is closed to visitors but you can see bits of it thanks to screens and
mirrors. The Parminters used glass, pottery and stones to supplement
the shells in creating charming decorations.

The ownership of the house has had some interesting twists and turns.
When Mary died in 1849, she stipulated that the property could only
be passed to unmarried female relatives, which was initially followed.
Then it somehow ended up with the Reverend Oswald Reichel, whose
widow tried to sell it to a developer, but a relative called Margaret
Tudor bought it and opened it to the public in 1935.

Because it was pretty much kept in the family, the furnishings and
trinkets belong to the place. And although not everything is exactly
as the Parminters had it, you still get a real sense of how harmonious
it must have been to live in a round house full of beautiful pictures
and treasures in a gorgeous setting.

Goat's Cheese, Pear and Walnut Scones

A sophisticated flavour combination. Choose a firm, fragrant pear for the best result.

450g self-raising flour
2 tsp baking powder
1 tbsp caster sugar
115g butter, cubed
130g goat's cheese, crumbled
80g Cheddar cheese, grated

1 pear, peeled and diced
60g walnuts, chopped
Pinch of salt and freshly ground
    black pepper
1 egg, beaten
Approx. 200ml milk

Preheat the oven to 190°C. Line a baking sheet with greaseproof paper.

Sift the flour with the baking powder and sugar into a mixing bowl. Add the butter and rub in using your fingertips until the mixture resembles fine crumbs.

Stir in most of the goat's cheese (reserving a little to top the scones), the Cheddar, diced pear, chopped walnuts, salt and pepper, then add the egg and enough milk to make a soft dough.

Turn out onto a lightly floured surface and roll out to about 4cm thick. Stamp out using a 7cm round cutter. Knead the trimmings together lightly, re-roll and stamp out more rounds. Place on the baking sheet. Brush the tops with milk and sprinkle with a little of the goat's cheese.

Bake for 15–20 minutes until risen and golden brown.

28

Moseley Old Hall (STAFFORDSHIRE)

Moseley Old Hall is an unusual National Trust property, in that it was given one chance of fame and it took it, a bit like Susan Boyle or Pippa Middleton. Over the course of two days in 1651 it went from being just someone's house near Cannock to securing notoriety for itself as the place that hid a king with a price on his head.

Charles II had marched south from Scotland with his army to reclaim the throne. However, he was roundly defeated at the Battle of Worcester on 3 September and went on the run. In the early hours of 8 September he arrived at Moseley Old Hall, bedraggled and tired. On his way to Moseley he had stayed at Boscobel House, where he had famously hidden in an oak tree while Roundhead soldiers searched for him nearby (thereby giving hundreds of pubs their name, The Royal Oak).

Moseley Old Hall had been built in 1600 and was owned by Thomas Whitgreave. Thomas was Catholic and had been hiding a priest, Father Huddleston, in a concealed space under a cupboard. Moseley's priest hole was also used by Charles II when troops arrived at the house – not looking for Charles, but to arrest Whitgreave. The priest hole and the four-poster bed where Charles slept can still be seen today.

Charles then left Moseley to continue on to Bristol, disguised as a servant. He eventually made it to the safety of France, thanks to men and women like Thomas Whitgreave. The story has a poignant and touching ending: when Charles II lay dying in 1685, Father Huddleston gave him the last rites.

Red Pepper, Onion and Cheese Scones

Colourful savoury scones, perfect to pack for a picnic.

500g self-raising flour
2 tsp baking powder
140g butter, cubed
½ red pepper, finely chopped

½ red onion, finely chopped
100g Cheddar cheese, grated
1 egg, beaten, plus extra to glaze
250ml milk

Preheat the oven to 210°C. Grease a baking sheet.

Sift the flour and baking powder into a mixing bowl. Add the butter and rub in using your fingertips until the mixture resembles fine crumbs. Stir in the red pepper, onion and cheese.

Add the beaten egg and then start to add the milk. Mixing with a round-bladed knife, keep adding milk until you have a soft dough. You may not need all the milk.

Turn out onto a floured surface and knead briefly, then roll out to about 3cm thick. Stamp out using a 7cm round cutter. Place on the baking sheet and brush the tops with beaten egg.

Bake for 10–12 minutes until risen and golden brown.

29

Anglesey Abbey and Lode Mill
(CAMBRIDGESHIRE)

Anglesey Abbey is believed to have been founded in 1135. It became a priory of Augustinian monks until the Dissolution of the Monasteries in the sixteeenth century. It then fell into the hands of various families: some lived there, some let it fall into disrepair. One owner was Thomas Hobson, who bought Anglesey in 1625. He used to hire out horses and would allow customers to 'choose' from only one horse, this being the origin of the phrase 'Hobson's choice'.

In 1926 it was bought by Huttleston Broughton, 1st Lord Fairhaven, and his brother as a convenient base for their stud and racing interests at nearby Newmarket. Fairhaven bequeathed Anglesey Abbey to the National Trust in 1966. It is presented as he left it; very much a country estate from the first half of the twentieth century. Only the dining room remains from the priory days – it was originally built in c1236. It's a sizeable house, full of art and ornaments, and there's even a gallery with Lord Fairhaven's extensive collection of pictures of Windsor Castle.

The highlight for me today, though, was the working mill. National Trust mills are always manned by the most enthusiastic, knowledgeable volunteers ever, which explains why we came away laden down with bags of flour 'milled just an hour ago'.

Roasted Shallot, Gruyère and Thyme Scones

Serve these wonderfully moist scones at a weekend brunch.

100g shallots, peeled	1 tsp cracked black pepper
A little olive oil	1 heaped tbsp chopped fresh thyme
450g self-raising flour	130g Gruyère cheese, grated
2 tsp baking powder	1 egg
115g unsalted butter, cubed	150ml milk, plus extra to brush
1 tsp sea salt	

Preheat the oven to 220°C. Line a baking sheet with greaseproof paper.

Place the shallots on a baking sheet, drizzle with a little olive oil and roast for 15–20 minutes. Leave to cool.

Sift the flour and baking powder into a large mixing bowl. Rub in the butter until the mixture resembles fine crumbs. Stir in the salt, pepper, thyme and 100g of the cheese. Chop the cooled shallots into small pieces and gently mix into the dry ingredients.

Combine the egg with the milk. Make a well in the centre of the dry ingredients and pour in the liquid. Mix to make a soft dough.

Turn out onto a lightly floured surface and knead very briefly to form a ball. Cut the dough in half. Form each half into a circle about 2.5cm thick, then cut into quarters to make four wedge-shaped scones. Place the scones on the lined baking sheet, brush lightly with milk and top each scone with some of the remaining cheese.

Bake for 12–15 minutes until well risen and golden brown. Transfer to a wire rack to cool slightly.

30

St Michael's Mount (Cornwall)

St Michael's Mount is one of the most popular National Trust properties, which is amazing considering it's fourteen miles from Land's End, so on hardly anyone's doorstep. Perhaps it's the causeway – there's something wonderful about a building that is accessible only by a road that disappears regularly into the sea. If you go to the Mount, I recommend you check the tide times.

As everyone knows, St Michael's Mount was created when the Cornubian batholith was formed following the cooling of magma 275 million years ago; it's likely that people have lived on the Mount since the Stone Age. The church, consecrated in 1144, is the oldest part of the building, and the Mount was once owned by the French monks of Mont St Michel, its Norman counterpart. The Mount is very durable: it survived an earthquake in 1275 and a mini-tsunami (three metres high) in 1755, which severely damaged the harbour.

A fascinating historical titbit is that the wife of the pretender Perkin Warbeck stayed there. Warbeck claimed to be one of the Princes in the Tower, and in 1497 raised an army in Cornwall to claim the throne from Henry VII. Mrs Warbeck stayed at St Michael's Mount for safety, while Perkin finally gave himself up as an imposter and met a predictably grisly end.

The St Aubyn family arrived in 1659 . . . and they'll be there until 2953! A descendant of the original owner, Colonel John St Aubyn, gave the Mount to the National Trust in 1954, but negotiated a 999-year lease for the family, who still live there today, in what is a very comfortable house.

Carrot and Coriander Scones

Top with cream cheese for a teatime treat or serve with soup at lunchtime.

500g self-raising flour
125g butter, cubed
115g grated carrot
25g fresh coriander, chopped

½ tsp ground cumin
Pinch of salt and freshly ground
    black pepper
180ml milk

Preheat the oven to 190°C. Line a baking sheet with greaseproof paper.

Sift the flour into a mixing bowl and, using your fingertips, rub in the butter until the mixture resembles fine crumbs.

Stir in the carrot, coriander, cumin, salt and pepper. Add the milk a little at a time, stirring with a round-bladed knife until you have a soft dough. You may not need all the milk.

Turn out onto a lightly floured surface and roll out to about 3cm thick. Stamp out using a 7cm round cutter. Knead the trimmings together lightly, re-roll and stamp out more rounds. Place on the baking sheet and brush the tops lightly with milk.

Bake for 15–20 minutes or until a knife inserted into the side of a scone comes out clean.

31

Dyffryn Gardens (Vale of Glamorgan)

If I had to pick a job from history that I would have hated, 'Victorian plant hunter' would be high on the list. Weeks of being thrown about on a rickety boat to some far-flung place; potentially being eaten by something (or someone) while you thrashed about in the undergrowth searching for specimens; lovingly drawing your findings; carefully storing them for the voyage home; then losing the lot when your ship got stuck on the Godwin Sands half a mile off Dover. I'd have taken my chances up a chimney, frankly.

Luckily the Victorians and Edwardians were a bit braver than me. Dyffryn Gardens in the Vale of Glamorgan was the creation of John Cory, a wealthy industrialist who sounds about as Victorian as it was possible to be; he was a coal-exporting teetotaller who gave a huge amount of money to charities and other causes.

John bought Dyffryn in 1891. Before that, it had been owned by a variety of people, including the fabulously named Bishop Oudaceous in the seventh century. John Cory started work on a new house almost immediately. His son, Reginald, later took a major interest in the gardens and worked with Thomas Mawson, a famous landscape architect of the time, to create a spectacular estate.

Reginald was particularly famous for his dahlias, but Dyffryn has many different elements to it. One of those elements is the Arboretum where Reg used to plant the trees and shrubs he had brought back from his plant-hunting expeditions in China, South Africa and the West Indies. Another is its beautiful themed garden rooms, including a Theatre Garden and a Pompeiian Garden, complete with columns, temple and fountain.

Beetroot Scones

Spread with soft goat's cheese and sprinkle with chopped walnuts to contrast with the vivid colour and earthy flavour of these scones.

225g self-raising flour
1 tsp baking powder
40g butter, cubed

4 cooked beetroots
Pinch of salt
3–4 tbsp milk

Preheat the oven to 220°C. Line a baking sheet with baking paper.

Sift the flour and baking powder into a mixing bowl. Add the butter and rub in until the mixture resembles fine crumbs.

Grate two of the beetroots and add to the mixture, along with the salt.

Cut the remaining beetroots into approx. 1cm cubes and add to the mixture, using a round-bladed knife to mix well. Gradually add the milk, stirring with the knife until you have a soft dough. You may not need all the milk; don't make it too sticky.

Turn out onto a lightly floured surface and knead briefly, then roll out to 2cm thick. Stamp out using a 4cm round cutter and place on the baking sheet.

Bake for 15 minutes until risen. Transfer to a wire rack to cool slightly before serving.

COOK'S TIP
If you like, you can add 100g grated mature cheese to the mix along with the cubed beetroots.

32

Chartwell (Kent)

Chartwell was the first National Trust property I ever visited. We did the same thing that hundreds of people do: we decided to go for a look round, got there and realised that the National Trust is a bit of a bargain if you join up instead of paying for a single visit.

Chartwell was the home of Sir Winston Churchill. He bought it in 1922 for £5000, much to the despair of his wife Clementine, who took one look at it and knew that it was going to be an expensive project.

Churchill employed the architect Philip Tilden to modernise the place, and although Clemmie was right and it did cause a lot of money worries, it acted as a sanctuary for the Churchills right up until he died in 1965. Clementine did not wish to live there after he passed away, so she worked with the National Trust to restore it to its pre-war glory, and that's how we see it today.

My second visit to Chartwell was inspired by them getting a new cat. It's a lovely little story. For his eighty-eighth birthday in 1962, Churchill was given a ginger cat, which he named Jock. The cat was so loved by Churchill that meals would not start until Jock was at the table. Churchill decreed that Chartwell should always have a marmalade cat with a white bib and four white socks named Jock in residence, and recently Jock VI arrived.

I only saw Jock VI distantly. I must have taken leave of my senses, expecting a cat to appear on demand. Cats don't do demand, unless they're doing the demanding. I know this, I have one in my home.

The spirit of Churchill definitely lives on in the house – if he walked in the door behind you, it wouldn't be a surprise – but it also has a strangely modern feel to it. It doesn't feel as 'preserved' as some other properties. It's also very much a home, despite the fact that several rooms are full of fascinating displays and artefacts. It's a fitting tribute to an exceptional man.

Horseradish Scones

Serve these small and spicy scones as canapés with a topping of crème fraîche, smoked salmon and chives.

250g self-raising flour
70g butter, cubed
Pinch of salt and freshly ground
   black pepper

2 tbsp horseradish sauce or
   10g fresh horseradish, grated
1 egg, beaten
Splash of milk

Preheat the oven to 200°C. Line a baking sheet with baking paper.

Sift the flour into a mixing bowl and add the butter, salt and pepper. Using your fingertips, rub the butter into the flour until the mixture resembles fine crumbs.

Make a well in the centre and add the horseradish and egg and just enough milk to make a soft dough.

Turn out onto a floured surface and roll out to about 2cm thick. Stamp out using a 4cm round cutter. Place on the baking sheet and lightly brush the tops with milk.

Bake for 10–15 minutes until risen and golden. Transfer to a wire rack to cool slightly before serving.

COOK'S TIP
Horseradish sauce varies greatly from brand to brand. You may need to add a little more if you prefer a strong flavour; alternatively, if using less horseradish sauce, you may need a little more milk.

Fruity Scones

33

Tredegar House (NEWPORT)

I do love a National Trust property that has an 'interesting' family attached to it and Tredegar (pronounced Tre-DEE-ga) doesn't disappoint.

The Tudor part of the house was built by John ap Morgan, who had supported Henry Tudor in 1485 and was rewarded with local land. The red-brick house we see today was built between 1664 and 1774 for William Morgan. William's second wife, Elizabeth Dayrell, repeatedly attacked him and was committed to Bedlam.

The Morgans thrived during the Industrial Revolution. Godfrey Morgan, who inherited in 1875, had been one of only two officers to survive the Charge of the Light Brigade (his horse, 'Sir Briggs', is buried in the garden). At its peak, Godfrey's income exceeded £1000 a day, which was a *lot* of money. His nephew Courtenay inherited and set about spending the above-mentioned fortune.

But it was Courtenay's son Evan who topped them all. This was a man who converted to Catholicism and became a Papal chamberlain, apparently unhindered by the fact that he was a) gay and b) a practitioner of the occult. He had many animals, including a baboon called Bimbo. Evan died and the house passed to his cousin John, who couldn't afford its upkeep, so he sold up to some nuns and moved to the South of France.

And that was the end of the Morgans at Tredegar. The house became a school, until the council bought the estate in 1974. The National Trust took on the lease in 2012 and have begun the process of restoring the place, starting with a £5 million roof replacement project (eek!). What a shame Evan spent all those millions on baboon food.

Cherry and Vanilla Scones

Simple-to-make scones with the comforting flavour of vanilla.

500g self-raising flour
40g caster sugar
55g butter, cubed

1 tsp vanilla extract
120ml milk
200g glacé cherries, quartered

Preheat the oven to 190°C. Grease a large baking sheet.

Sift the flour and sugar into a mixing bowl, add the butter and rub in until the mixture resembles fine crumbs.

Mix the vanilla extract with the milk and gradually add to the dry ingredients, mixing with a round-bladed knife until you have a soft dough. You may not need all the milk. Add the cherries and mix briefly to distribute evenly.

Turn out onto a lightly floured surface and roll out to about 3cm thick. Stamp out using a 7cm round fluted cutter, place on the baking sheet and brush the tops with a little milk.

Bake for 15–18 minutes until well risen and golden brown.

34

Rufford Old Hall (Lancashire)

If any TV channel is looking for a stately-home-based Sunday night drama to replace 'Downton Abbey', they could do worse than tell the story of Rufford Old Hall.

It has an amazing history, full of unusual twists. The estate was owned by the Hesketh family from the late thirteenth century. Thomas Hesketh, who inherited in 1491, divorced his first wife after she became pregnant by somebody else (he got to keep her land, though). He married again but all of his sons died young, so he left the estate to Robert, his eldest son by his mistress.

Somehow, Robert managed to fight off the other non-illegitimate claimants and it was he who built the magnificent manor that we see at Rufford today.

After Robert came his son, Sir Thomas Hesketh, who kept a company of musicians and actors. He unknowingly secured fame for Rufford Old Hall by probably employing a seventeen-year-old actor called William Shakespeare for a few months in 1581.

The brick wing of the house was built in 1662. Then in the 1720s, another Thomas Hesketh created the East Wing by relocating a structure from Holmeswood Hall to Rufford.

The family had moved out of Rufford Old Hall around 1760. In the 1820s, Thomas Henry Hesketh moved back in and remodelled it, but it was occupied sporadically before being handed to the National Trust in 1936.

Cherry and Almond Scones

Studded with cherries and subtly flavoured with a hint of almonds, these are perfect for afternoon tea.

450g self-raising flour
½ tsp baking powder
100g butter, cubed
75g caster sugar
175g glacé cherries, roughly chopped

1 egg, beaten, plus extra to glaze
A few drops of almond essence
150–180ml milk
2–3 tbsp flaked almonds

Preheat the oven to 190°C. Grease a large baking sheet.

Sift the flour and baking powder into a mixing bowl. Using your fingertips, rub in the butter. Add the sugar, cherries, egg, almond essence and enough milk to make a soft but not sticky dough. Knead lightly until smooth.

Turn out onto a lightly floured surface and roll out to about 3cm thick. Stamp out using a 7cm round cutter and place on the baking sheet. Brush the tops with beaten egg and sprinkle with flaked almonds.

Bake for about 20 minutes until well risen, firm and golden. Transfer to a wire rack to cool. Serve with butter or clotted cream and jam.

35

Ightham Mote (KENT)

Ightham Mote (pronounced Item) is 700 years old and has the only Grade I listed dog kennel in existence, which is a half-timbered affair built in 1891 for a St Bernard called Dido. If that alone doesn't make it worth paying for National Trust membership, then I don't know what does. (Disappointingly, Dido didn't get much publicity. There was no one leaping about in a big dog costume and no plaque explaining her life and times.)

Ightham is a little treasure of a place and the house and its contents were bequeathed to the National Trust by Charles Henry Robinson in 1985. He was an American, who purchased it in 1953 having seen an advertisement in an old issue of *Country Life*. No one is exactly sure who built it, but the materials used in the tower and the Great Hall date back to the fourteenth century. It's been extended and chopped and changed over the years but has somehow retained a sense of wholeness. Like many other properties, you discover rooms from a medieval Great Hall to a chapel consecrated in 1633 to bedrooms refurbished in the twentieth century, but somehow it feels right at Ightham. Maybe it's because, being surrounded by a moat, it exists in its own little bubble of time.

The celebrated architectural historian Sir Nikolaus Pevsner described it as 'the most complete small medieval manor house in the country', and if anyone should know, he should. Among its curiosities is a 'porter's squint', a narrow slit in the wall through which the porter could vet any visitors before opening the gate. It's one of the many things worth making the trip to Ightham for.

Zesty Lemon Scones

A lovely summery alternative to the traditional scone.

500g self-raising flour
1 tsp baking powder
115g caster sugar
115g salted butter, cubed
Grated zest and juice of 2 lemons
1 egg, beaten
100–150ml milk

TO DECORATE
100g icing sugar
Juice of ½ to 1 lemon

Preheat the oven to 200°C. Line a baking sheet with baking paper.

Sift the flour, baking powder and sugar into a mixing bowl, add the butter and, using your fingertips, rub in until the mixture resembles fine crumbs. Stir in the lemon zest and juice.

Add the beaten egg and then gradually add the milk, mixing with a round-bladed knife until you have a soft dough. You may not need all the milk.

Turn out onto a lightly floured surface and knead briefly, then roll out to about 3cm thick. Stamp out using a 7cm round fluted cutter. Place on the baking sheet and brush the tops lightly with milk.

Bake for 15–20 minutes until golden. Transfer to a wire rack to cool.

To decorate, sift the icing sugar into a bowl. Add the lemon juice, a little at a time, and stir until the icing has a dropping consistency. Spoon the icing over the cooled scones. Serve with clotted cream and lemon curd.

36

Nymans (WEST SUSSEX)

If a heritage-loving alien arrived on Earth and wanted to be shown one property that sums up the National Trust, I'd take it to Nymans. It has everything: extensive gardens; a picturesque ruin; and a mock medieval house that you can go inside and see where an Edwardian Englishwoman lived.

I was actually expecting Nymans to be a bit of a sad place. The original manor house and gardens were bought by Ludwig Messel in the 1890s. His son Leonard remodelled it, creating a striking mansion (designed by Walter Tapper and the magnificently named Norman Evill, who sound like they should have been arch-enemies). But then it burned down. The ruined bit might look lovely and romantic now but imagine it on that February morning in 1947 when it was a smouldering pile of rubble. Leonard never went back and the National Trust took over Nymans after his death in 1953. His daughter Anne (who was the mother of Antony Armstrong-Jones, Princess Margaret's husband) lived there in some capacity until she died in 1992.

But Nymans isn't sad at all. The ruin is beautiful, while the rooms you can enter give you some idea of how amazing it must have been to have lived here during its twenty-year heyday. Nymans is famous for its gardens and they are indeed stunning, a pertinent reminder of how landscape gardeners are unique, in that they're always designing and planting for the future – and not just for next spring, but for twenty or thirty years' time, or even beyond their lifetimes. It was badly damaged in the Great Storm of 1987, losing 486 mature trees, and restoration continues today.

Orange and Cranberry Scones

Fragrant with orange and bejewelled with cranberries, these would be charming made with heart-shaped cutters for an engagement or wedding anniversary party.

500g self-raising flour
140g butter, cubed
90g caster sugar
125g dried cranberries

Grated zest and juice of 1 large
   orange
1 egg, beaten, plus extra to glaze
100–120ml milk

Preheat the oven to 210°C. Grease a baking sheet.

Sift the flour into a mixing bowl and, using your fingertips, rub in the butter until the mixture resembles fine crumbs. Stir in the sugar, cranberries and orange zest and juice.

Add the beaten egg and then start to add the milk, mixing with a round-bladed knife until you have a soft dough. You may not need all the milk.

Turn out onto a floured surface and knead briefly, then roll out to about 3cm thick. Stamp out using a 7cm round cutter. Place on the baking sheet and brush the tops with beaten egg.

Bake for 10–12 minutes until risen and golden brown.

37

Wordsworth House and Garden
(Cumbria)

'I wandered lonely as a cloud' is the only thing I knew about William Wordsworth until my visit to Wordsworth House and Garden. And when I say the only thing, I mean it. I didn't even know the second line of that poem – I knew the word 'daffodils' was in there somewhere but that was it. And I have a confession: I studied English Literature at university; I did a *whole term* on the Romantic poets. It's beyond embarrassing.

The house itself was built between 1670 and 1690. John Wordsworth, dad of William, moved there in 1765 – it came rent-free as part of his job as agent for Sir James Lowther. William was the second child born to John and his wife Ann, arriving in 1770, followed by his literary sister Dorothy in 1771. Ann Wordsworth died in 1778, aged just 31 – this had a big impact on the family, with Dorothy being packed off to relatives in Halifax. John died just five years later in 1783, upon which the house was given back to Sir James and the boys were also sent to live with relatives.

I now know that in his great autobiographical poem, *The Prelude*, William talks about his happy childhood growing up by the River Derwent, which runs behind the house. I must admit, I expected Wordsworth to have grown up in a tiny cottage somewhere, not in a sizeable house on a main street in Cockermouth. But the house is great: you get a real sense of what life would have been like for him.

Wordsworth House was badly flooded in December 2015. The water was three feet deep and yet – typical of the dedicated National Trust staff – the house still managed to open in March as planned.

Apple and Raisin Scones

An autumnal twist on classic fruit scones.

500g self-raising flour	1 apple, peeled and diced
70g caster sugar	100g raisins
Pinch of salt	250ml milk
90g butter, cubed	

Preheat the oven to 220°C. Line a baking sheet with greaseproof paper.

Sift the flour, sugar and salt into a mixing bowl and, using your fingertips, rub in the butter, working quickly and lightly. Stir in the apple and raisins.

Make a well in the centre and pour in the milk. Mixing quickly and lightly with a round-bladed knife, bring the ingredients together to make a soft dough.

Turn out onto a lightly floured surface and shape into a rough circle, pressing down very lightly until it is about 3cm thick. Stamp out using a 7cm round cutter. Place the scones on the baking sheet, leaving space around them so there is room for them to rise. Brush the tops lightly with milk, then dust with flour.

Bake for 15–20 minutes until risen and golden. Transfer to a wire rack to cool slightly. Serve warm, with butter.

38

Smallhythe Place (KENT)

One of my favourite things about the National Trust is that you go along not knowing anything at all about a person and you come away fascinated by them. I definitely recognised the name Ellen Terry before my trip to Smallhythe. I just couldn't think who she was.

It turns out that Ellen Terry was a very famous Victorian actress. She was born in Coventry in 1847 to theatrical parents, so naturally she and her sister Kate followed suit. The artist G.F. Watts painted Ellen and Kate, and Ellen married him when he was forty-six and she was seventeen, but they separated within a year – she went on to have several 'relationships' and married again twice, while her acting career went from strength to strength. She was created a dame in 1925 and died in 1928.

She first saw Smallhythe in the late 1890s when she was driving around Kent with Henry Irving and asked the old shepherd living in the house to tell her when he was ready to sell. In 1899 she received a postcard with three words on it 'House for Sale' – and that was that.

The house at Smallhythe was built in the first half of the sixteenth century and was the Port House to the shipyard – the River Rother used to be navigable as far as Smallhythe before the water receded. The National Trust took over the house in 1939. There are hundreds of pictures and photographs of Ellen Terry around the house, as well as a Costume Room and stacks of memorabilia. There is also an actual working theatre there, where many famous actors have appeared. (I tried to resist saying 'More cheese, Gromit?' when I saw the name Peter Sallis, but failed.)

Apple and Cinnamon Scones

The irresistible aroma of cinnamon fills the kitchen as you bake these scones.

500g self-raising flour
140g butter, cubed
90g caster sugar
1 large apple, peeled and diced
2 tsp ground cinnamon

1 egg, beaten, plus extra to glaze
Approx. 200ml milk

Preheat the oven to 210°C. Grease a baking sheet.

Sift the flour into a mixing bowl and, using your fingertips, rub in the butter until the mixture resembles fine crumbs. Stir in the sugar, apple and cinnamon.

Add the beaten egg and then start to add the milk, mixing with a round-bladed knife until you have a soft dough. You may not need all the milk.

Turn out onto a lightly floured surface and knead briefly, then roll out to about 3cm thick. Stamp out using a 7cm round cutter. Place on the baking sheet and brush the tops with beaten egg.

Bake for 10–12 minutes until risen and golden brown.

39

Avebury (WILTSHIRE)

Avebury village is sort-of famous for its standing stones – not mega-famous and ostentatious, more Charlie Watts to Stonehenge's Mick Jagger.

The stones are part of Avebury henge; originally there would have been around a hundred stones in the Outer Circle at Avebury, but today there are thirty-six standing within the henge. Fifteen have remained upright throughout time, since 2,600 BC or so, the other twenty-one were put back up by an archaeologist called Alexander Keiller during his excavations in the 1930s – they'd either fallen over or been buried. Nobody knows for sure why the stones were put there, but it doesn't really matter – it's still a fascinating experience.

The accompanying museum is good. You can learn how Alexander was heir to the Keiller marmalade business and spent his fortune on all sorts of interests, but mainly women and archaeology.

Avebury Manor, just a five-minute walk from the stones, is thought to date from the 1500s. It was the star of the 2011 BBC/National Trust collaboration *The Manor Reborn*, where part of the interior – which Keiller had used as a base for his excavations – was refurbished by experts and volunteers in four heritage styles: Tudor, Georgian, Victorian and Pre-War Modern. They also created a Victorian kitchen garden.

I ended my trip with a quick detour up the road to Silbury Hill. Silbury is thirty-seven metres high, the largest prehistoric mound in Europe, and was created in 2400–2000 BC. You stand there wondering what on earth could be inside it – aliens, vast ancient treasures, a Bond villain? – until you read the signs, which explain that when archaeologists tried to tunnel into it, all they found was mud. And as a result of the tunnels the whole thing started eroding, so they had to fill them in and go away again.

Lemon and Coconut Scones

The scone that thinks it's a cake.

500g self-raising flour
125g caster sugar
125g salted butter, cubed
100g desiccated coconut
Grated zest and juice of 2 lemons
Approx. 140ml milk

1 tbsp lemon curd
1 egg

To decorate (optional)
1 tbsp lemon curd
2 tbsp desiccated coconut

Preheat the oven to 190°C. Line a baking sheet with greaseproof paper.

Sift the flour and sugar into a mixing bowl, add the butter and rub in until it resembles fine crumbs. Add the coconut and lemon zest and juice and mix briefly.

Pour the milk into a jug, add the lemon curd, crack in the egg and stir briefly. Make a well in the centre of the dry mixture and gradually pour in the liquid, adding enough to draw all the mixture into a damp dough but not enough to make it sloppy and wet.

Turn out onto a lightly floured surface and roll out to about 4cm thick. Stamp out using an 8cm round fluted cutter and place on the baking sheet. Push the trimmings together, re-roll and stamp out more rounds.

Bake for 18–20 minutes until golden brown. Transfer to a wire rack to cool.

If you want to decorate the scones, mix the lemon curd with a dash of hot water and brush over the scones, then sprinkle with desiccated coconut. Serve with butter and lemon curd.

40

Greys Court (OXFORDSHIRE)

When I had a preparatory look on the Greys Court website I saw that they have a 'rare Tudor donkey wheel', which sounded intriguing. (I must admit that I didn't actually know what a Tudor donkey wheel was. I think I was hoping that there might be a 500-year-old Tudor donkey attached to it.)

Greys Court is a lovely little place. It was built in the sixteenth century and bought in 1937 by Sir Felix and Lady Elizabeth Brunner, who made it their family home. Lady Brunner died in 2003 and the house is presented pretty much as she left it. (Two interesting factoids about Lady Brunner: she was the granddaughter of the noted Victorian actor-manager Sir Henry Irving; and she founded the Keep Britain Tidy group.) There are walled gardens at Greys and in the grounds is a fourteenth-century tower that's the only thing left of a medieval castle.

But the undoubted highlight for me was the Tudor donkey wheel. A picture on the wall brought me up to speed pretty quickly as to what a donkey wheel does – it's basically like a hamster wheel for donkeys, except that hamsters don't generally power the lifting of buckets of water from a well. (And the donkeys don't go on the wheel at 3 a.m. when everyone is trying to sleep and all they can hear is Fluffy going like the clappers, until one day Fluffy 'escapes' and that's the end of that.)

The ingenious donkey wheel at Greys Court was in operation from Tudor times right through to 1914. The donkeys would hear the noise that signalled that the bucket had reached the top of the pulley and would stop, be turned around and then walk the other way so that the next buckets were lowered/raised. Ingenious!

Peach, Vanilla and Poppy Seed Scones

Summer has arrived. But don't worry if the weather is less than peachy: you can use tinned peaches in place of the fresh ones.

500g plain flour
2 tsp baking powder
100g caster sugar
125g butter, cubed
3 small fresh peaches, roughly
    chopped

1 tsp poppy seeds
½ tsp vanilla extract
1 egg, beaten
100ml milk

Preheat the oven to 190°C. Line a baking sheet with greaseproof paper.

Sift the flour, baking powder and sugar into a mixing bowl and then, using your fingertips, rub in the butter until the mixture resembles fine crumbs.

Stir in the chopped peaches, poppy seeds and vanilla extract. Add the egg and enough milk to make a soft dough.

Turn out onto a lightly floured surface and roll out to about 4cm thick. Stamp out using a 7cm round cutter. Push the trimmings together, knead lightly, re-roll and stamp out more rounds. Place on the baking sheet and brush the tops lightly with milk.

Bake for 15–20 minutes or until golden brown. Best served with clotted cream and apricot jam.

41

—

Dunham Massey (Cheshire)

The original house at Dunham Massey was built by 'Old' Sir George Booth in 1600. The Booths were heavily involved in politics during the Civil War, just about staying on the right side of things as the tides turned. George's great-grandson, Henry Booth, was made 1st Earl of Warrington by William III, but it all turned sour and Henry ended up deeply in debt. His son George married a wealthy heiress – although the marriage was unhappy, it saved Dunham Massey. George unusually passed Dunham to his daughter, Lady Mary Booth, who married the 4th Earl of Stamford. Their son, George Harry Grey, became 5th Earl of Stamford and Warrington.

The 7th Earl was quite a character: he first married a bedmaker's daughter called Bessy and then a circus performer called Catherine Cocks. She was rejected by local society, so the Greys left Dunham and did not return for fifty years. The 9th Earl, William Grey, inherited Dunham in a sorry state in 1905. He started to restore the place in 1906, but died suddenly in 1910 when his son Roger was just thirteen. Roger eventually continued the restoration of Dunham but never married and gave the 3,000-acre estate to the National Trust in 1976.

One of the most fascinating aspects of the house is its use during the First World War. In 1917 the Greys agreed to turn it into an auxiliary hospital for injured troops. Dunham Massey was approached because it was near Manchester and only three people lived there at the time (Lady Stamford, her son Roger, the 10th Earl, and her daughter, Lady Jane). Lady Stamford became the Commandant of the hospital, while Lady Jane worked as a nurse. Rooms were converted into wards and an operating theatre was set up at the bottom of the staircase. It's all a far cry from the grandeur of the place today.

Blackberry and Apple Scones

Make the most of your hedgerow treasures with these juicy scones.

500g self-raising flour
125g soft brown sugar
1 tsp ground cinnamon
125g salted butter, cubed

2 small apples, peeled and diced
175ml milk
1 egg
125g fresh or frozen blackberries

Preheat the oven to 190°C. Line a baking sheet with greaseproof paper.

Sift the flour, sugar and cinnamon into a mixing bowl, add the butter and rub in until it resembles fine crumbs. Add the diced apples and mix briefly to distribute them evenly.

Pour the milk into a jug, crack in the egg and stir to mix. Make a well in the centre of the dry ingredients and gradually pour in the liquid, adding enough to draw all the mixture into a damp dough but not enough to make it sloppy and wet.

Add the blackberries and stir through gently.

Turn out onto a lightly floured surface and roll out to about 3cm thick. Stamp out using a 7cm round fluted cutter and place on the baking sheet. Gently knead the trimmings together, re-roll and stamp out more rounds.

Bake for 15–20 minutes until risen and springy to the touch. Transfer to a wire rack to cool slightly. Serve warm with blackcurrant jam and clotted cream.

42

Sutton Hoo (Suffolk)

Sutton Hoo is just the sort of place I would have loved to have visited on a school trip but never got the chance. It shot to stardom in 1939, when local archaeologist Basil Brown unearthed the remains of a massive wooden ship. Basil had been invited there by land-owner Edith Pretty, who had often wondered what the mounds on her land contained. In 1938, he had explored a few of the mounds and found evidence of a burial site, which had clearly already been plundered. The next year he returned to excavate further and soon uncovered iron rivets that suggested an Anglo-Saxon ship burial. As Basil continued, he was staggered at the size of the boat that he was uncovering.

Surprisingly, this burial chamber had *not* been breached, and the team were soon uncovering gold jewellery, coins, weapons, leather and more. The most famous item is the great iron helmet, which is now in the British Museum along with many of the other treasures. The burial site is thought to be that of King Raedwald, who died in AD 625.

Sutton Hoo is the gift that keeps on giving – in 1992, another mound was excavated and a double grave was found, containing a young man and a horse. The on-site museum tells the story very well and there are replicas of some of the finds, plus a treasury containing genuine artefacts. And then you can walk around the actual burial site itself. I did at this point think of some of the kids that I was at school with and how they'd probably have treated the mounds like an adventure playground, so it was probably just as well we didn't get to go.

Fig, Orange and Walnut Scones

Try these split and filled with cream cheese, as an alternative to icing them.

500g self-raising flour
100g caster sugar
125g butter, cubed
Grated zest of 1 orange
2 dried figs, chopped
30g walnuts, chopped
Approx. 150ml milk

TO DECORATE (OPTIONAL)
100g icing sugar
A little fresh orange juice

Preheat the oven to 190°C. Line a baking sheet with greaseproof paper.

Sift the flour and sugar into a mixing bowl and, using your fingertips, rub in the butter until the mixture resembles fine crumbs. Add the orange zest, figs and walnuts and stir to combine.

Add enough milk to make a soft dough and knead briefly until smooth.

Turn out onto a lightly floured surface and roll out to about 3cm thick. Stamp out using a 7cm round cutter and place on the baking sheet.

Bake for 12–18 minutes until risen and golden. Transfer to a wire rack to cool.

To decorate, sift the icing sugar into a bowl. Add orange juice, a little at a time, and stir until the icing has a dropping consistency. Drizzle over the cooled scones.

43

Clouds Hill (Dorset)

If there was an award for National Trust Property That Doesn't Look Very Interesting But Turns Out To Be Brilliant, then Clouds Hill would win it. First impressions were not good. Remember, we're talking National Trust. Clouds Hill could have been a castle; it could have been a manor house; it could have been a hill. In fact, it's a little hovel with no windows. Why, I asked myself, would the National Trust want to own it?

The answer is Lawrence of Arabia. The great T.E. Lawrence used this little place as his rural retreat from 1923 until his untimely death in 1935. He was born in 1888 at Tremadoc in Wales. In 1915 he was posted to the British Military Intelligence office in Cairo. He became an expert on Arabia and in 1922 published *The Seven Pillars of Wisdom*, an account of his experiences.

Back in England he rented a little ramshackle woodsman's cottage called Clouds Hill, where he could write and listen to music. He received many illustrious visitors there, including E.M. Forster and Thomas Hardy. He eventually bought Clouds Hill, loaning it out to friends while in India, before returning in 1929 to begin remodelling the house – it was completed in 1934 and remains the same today. The following year, he died after he swerved his motorbike to avoid some cyclists.

The rooms at Clouds Hill are compelling. The house somehow manages to be austere and yet cosy at the same time; my favourite feature was the enormous gramophone.

Apricot Scones

Delicate fruity scones for a spring or summer treat.

500g self-raising flour
140g butter, cubed
90g sugar
125g dried apricots, chopped

1 tsp vanilla extract (optional)
1 egg, beaten, plus extra to glaze
200ml milk

Preheat the oven to 210°C. Grease a baking sheet.

Sift the flour into a mixing bowl and, using your fingertips, rub in the butter until the mixture resembles fine crumbs. Stir in the sugar, apricots and vanilla.

Add the beaten egg and then start to add the milk, mixing with a round-bladed knife until you have a soft dough. You may not need all the milk.

Turn out onto a floured surface and knead briefly, then roll out to about 3cm thick. Stamp out using a 7cm round cutter. Place on the baking sheet and brush the tops with beaten egg.

Bake for 10–12 minutes until risen and golden brown. Serve with clotted cream and apricot jam.

44

Tatton Park (CHESHIRE)

Although Tatton Park is owned by the National Trust, it's run by
Cheshire East Council. But don't panic, Trust members, because:
a) it's still free for you to get in; and b) they run it very well, hosting
over 100 events every year, including the Moscow State Circus and the
intriguingly titled 'Pigs Galore'.

Tatton Park was owned by the Egerton family from 1598 to 1958.
The house you see today was completed in 1716, and then extended
by various Egertons over the years. A lot of country houses have
an up-and-down history, where one owner does loads of good work
and then the next fritters everything away, leaving someone else to
pick up the pieces. But the Egertons all did something positive to the
place, and they seem to have remained financially solvent, which must
have helped.

Tatton Park Gardens are stunning. There's a really good map
that directs you round the various elements: a beautiful Italian
garden right outside the house, a kitchen garden, a rose garden,
a Japanese garden, an arboretum . . . you name it and Tatton has
it. The park around the mansion covers 2,000 acres; it's been a deer
park since 1290 and there are still red and fallow deer wandering
about (probably not the same ones). Landscape gardener Humphry
Repton was involved in planning the park – he prepared a list of
recommendations in 1791, which included improving the water
features. Today there are two nice lakes, which help make it a
pleasant park to walk through, and it was very busy with joggers,
walkers, dogs, cyclists and picnickers when I visited; it's clearly a big
part of the local community.

Lemon and Cranberry Scones

Tangy lemon and tart cranberries give these scones a light, fresh taste.

300g plain flour
300g self-raising flour
2 tsp baking powder
1 tbsp caster sugar
Pinch of salt

170g unsalted butter, cubed
Grated zest of 3 lemons
60g dried cranberries
300ml milk
1 egg, beaten (optional)

Preheat the oven to 190°C. Line a baking sheet with greaseproof paper.

Sift the flours, baking powder, sugar and salt into a mixing bowl. Add the butter and rub in until it resembles fine crumbs. Stir in the lemon zest and cranberries.

Add three-quarters of the milk and mix until you have a sticky dough, being careful not to overmix. You may need to add a little more milk.

Turn out onto a lightly floured surface and roll out to about 3cm thick. Dip a 7cm round cutter in flour and stamp out rounds, flouring the cutter before each cut. Place the rounds on the baking sheet and brush the tops lightly with milk or beaten egg.

Bake for 15–20 minutes until risen and golden. Serve with clotted cream and lemon curd.

45

Hanbury Hall & Gardens (Worcestershire)

Hanbury Hall was built at the beginning of the eighteenth century, and externally, it hasn't really changed since. It was passed down through generations of the Vernon family, who all look very sombre and had extremely officious jobs.

Then it gets interesting: In 1776 Emma Vernon married Henry Cecil, heir to the 9th Earl of Exeter, but fell in love with the local curate, William Sneyd. After a secret affair, she confessed all to Henry, who gave her an ultimatum. However, when Henry took her to say her final goodbyes to her departing curate, she waited until Henry's back was turned and then escaped out of a window so she could run off to Portugal with Sneyd.

Henry was devastated and moved to a smallholding in Shropshire, calling himself John Jones. He fell in love with Sarah, a sixteen-year-old farmer's daughter, and married her – bigamously. He later divorced Emma and remarried Sarah properly. Sneyd and Emma also married but Sneyd died two years later. Emma returned to the Hanbury area, marrying a local lawyer. When Henry died, she moved back into Hanbury Hall.

Hanbury Hall is lovely. The highlight of the interior is the Great Staircase, which was painted by Sir James Thornhill for Thomas Vernon. It was good practice for Sir James, who went on to paint the cupola of St Paul's Cathedral. The gardens are beautiful too, and include a mushroom house.

Finally, a nugget from the local church. According to the guidebook, the bells of St Mary the Virgin can often be heard on Radio 4 as the bells of St Stephen's in Ambridge!

Blueberry and Lemon Scones

Fresh blueberries are available all year round; why not try them in these lemon-scented scones?

500g self-raising flour
125g caster sugar
125g butter, cubed
Grated zest of 1 lemon
100g blueberries
Approx. 150ml milk

TO DECORATE
100g icing sugar
A little lemon juice

Preheat the oven to 190°C. Line a baking sheet with greaseproof paper.

Sift the flour and sugar into a mixing bowl and, using your fingertips, rub in the butter until the mixture resembles fine crumbs. Add the lemon zest and blueberries and stir to combine.

Add enough milk to make a soft dough and knead briefly until smooth.

Turn out onto a lightly floured surface and roll out to about 3cm thick. Stamp out using a 7cm round cutter and place on the baking sheet.

Bake for 12–18 minutes until risen and golden. Transfer to a wire rack to cool.

To decorate, sift the icing sugar into a bowl. Add lemon juice, a little at a time, and stir until the icing has a dropping consistency. Drizzle over the cooled scones.

Festive
Scones

46

Nuffield Place (OXFORDSHIRE)

If you drew a Venn diagram and put the National Trust in one circle and 'Top Gear' in the other, the bit in the middle would say Nuffield Place. For this is where Lord Nuffield, founder of Morris Motor Cars, lived for thirty years until he died in 1963.

I'm not fascinated by cars or Jeremy Clarkson, but Lord Nuffield, aka William Morris (no, not *that* one), was a remarkable man. He started a bicycle repair business, aged just 16, in a shed at the back of his parents' home. This later developed into a business designing custom built bikes; by 1901 he had a shop on Oxford's High Street.

He moved onto motorcycles and then cars. He wanted to build a car that was affordable, and he did – the two-seater Morris Oxford was launched in 1913. The four-seater Morris Cowley followed, and eventually the legendary Morris Minor.

But you'll be disappointed if you're expecting to see loads of cars at Nuffield Place. The only car on show is Lady Nuffield's Wolseley – Morris bought the Wolseley firm in 1927 when it went bust.

The house is very much the star of the show; although it's roomy, it's a very modest house for a multi-millionaire industrialist. That unshowiness says an awful lot about Morris's personality. He preferred to give his millions away. He funded the Oxford college that bears his name and he gave generously to medical causes.

The whole place is down-to-earth. In his bedroom there's a wardrobe that opens up to reveal a little workshop, allowing him to fix clocks and other household items when he couldn't sleep at night. I was just leaving the room when I overheard the guide tell another visitor 'and there's his appendix right there on the shelf of course', so I had to scoot back in for another look. And sure enough, there it was.

Christmas Pudding Scones

A creative way to use leftover Christmas pudding.

450g self-raising flour
55g caster sugar
½ tsp mixed spice
55g butter, cubed

125g leftover Christmas pudding,
  broken into tiny pieces
250ml milk
1 tbsp brandy (optional)

Preheat the oven to 190°C. Lightly oil a baking sheet.

Sift the flour, sugar and spice into a mixing bowl, add the butter and rub in until it resembles fine crumbs. Stir in the Christmas pudding.

Make a well in the centre, add half the milk and the brandy, if using, then gradually mix in enough of the remaining milk to make a soft dough. Knead lightly.

Turn out onto a lightly floured surface and roll out to about 3cm thick. Stamp out using a 7cm round fluted cutter and place on the baking sheet. Gently knead the trimmings together, re-roll and stamp out more rounds. Brush the tops lightly with the remaining milk.

Bake for 15–20 minutes until golden brown and a knife inserted into the side of a scone comes out clean. Transfer to a wire rack to cool slightly. Serve warm, split and buttered or spread with a little brandy or rum butter.

COOK'S TIP
If you like, sprinkle a little ground cinnamon and caster sugar over the scones just before they go into the oven.

47

Dunwich Heath (SUFFOLK)

I love National Trust guidebooks. I always read them after I get home, though, and this has its dangers. They invariably contain some little factoid that would have been useful when you were on-site, so you find yourself wailing 'I didn't know there was a crypt containing the bones of 1,000 peasants!' or 'I didn't see the carousel that plays "Bat Out Of Hell!"' (I did see one of those once).

I bought a guidebook at Dunwich Heath and, sure enough, there it was on page five, the stop-you-in-your-tracks fact: by 2070, much of Dunwich will be gone. The beautiful coastguard cottages (which house the tea-room and shop), the approach road, the village – the coast will have eroded and it'll all have plopped down into the sea. And that, my friends, is a very sobering thought.

Dunwich itself is an absolutely beautiful spot. It's in between Southwold and Aldeburgh on the Suffolk coast and is tucked away in its own little corner. At the time of the Domesday Book, Dunwich was twice the size of Ipswich but it was gradually lost to coastal erosion, which continues today at a rate of 1 metre per year. The heath is rare coastal lowland heath (thanks, guidebook) and is home to Dartford warblers, adders, and other rare species that the National Trust works hard to conserve and protect.

The beach is perfect for walking – in fact there are countless walks around the area to burn some calories. Which is lucky, as Dunwich Heath is a shrine for scone lovers with its regular 'sconeathons', at which up to 1,000 scones of twenty different varieties are avidly consumed.

Stollen Scones

Just like the traditional German Christmas bread, these scones have a marzipan middle.

500g self-raising flour
125g soft light brown sugar
1 tsp ground nutmeg
2 tsp mixed spice
125g butter, cubed
50g mixed peel
60g sultanas
50g glacé cherries, finely chopped
1 piece of stem ginger, finely chopped

15g flaked almonds
25g walnut pieces
1 tsp almond essence
1 egg, beaten
175ml milk
120g marzipan
25g unsalted butter, melted
100g icing sugar

Preheat the oven to 190°C. Line a baking sheet with greaseproof paper.

Sift the flour, sugar and spices into a mixing bowl, add the butter and rub into fine crumbs. Add the fruit and nuts and stir briefly.

Make a well in the centre, add the almond essence and the egg and gradually pour in enough milk to make a soft dough.

Turn out onto a lightly floured surface and roll out to about 4cm thick. Stamp out using an 8cm round cutter and place on the baking sheet.

Divide the marzipan into small balls, about 2cm in diameter. Push a ball into the base of each scone and then use some of the remaining dough to cover the marzipan so that it is encased in the scone. Gently knead the trimmings together, re-roll and repeat the process.

Bake for 18–20 minutes until risen and springy to the touch. Transfer to a wire rack to cool slightly. Brush with melted butter and dredge with icing sugar.

48

South Foreland Lighthouse (KENT)

You have to work for it – it's a forty-minute walk from the White Cliffs of Dover Visitor Centre, although there's a minibus on Sundays – but it's 100% worth the effort.

Beacons have been placed on the cliffs for centuries, but the current lighthouse was built in the 1840s. It's positioned on the Dover cliffs because of the treacherous Goodwin Sands which lie three miles out to sea. The Goodwin Sands were known as 'the shippe swallower' in olden days, because the ten-mile sandbank is made of quicksand. The wrecks of 2,000 ships lie out there; one storm sank fifty vessels in 1703. The lighthouse was originally lit by oil until electricity arrived in 1872.

The volunteer who led us around the lighthouse was called Martin and he must be a serious contender for National Trust Tour Guide of the Year. He was brilliant. If you had told me I would listen enraptured to a man explaining the traffic patterns of the Strait of Dover, I would have thought you were mad. When I win the lottery I am going to offer Martin a job following me around explaining things; 'Martin, how has Greece ended up in this financial pickle?' 'Martin, how can I delete people on Facebook without them knowing?', etc, etc.

He told us that the lighthouse was decommissioned in 1988 and Trinity House (which runs our lighthouses) insisted on taking out all the apparatus because they weren't 100% certain that the National Trust wouldn't switch it on one day and cause mayhem among the ferries in the Channel. It was put back in eventually and the light was turned on for one night only for the jubilee in 2012. Apparently the ferries were tooting their horns as they went past. Brilliant.

Mulled Scones

Make your own mulled wine or buy it ready-made for these spicy scones.

100g sultanas
50g mixed peel
175ml mulled wine
450g self-raising flour
1 tsp baking powder
3 heaped tsp mixed spice
115g unsalted butter, cubed

85g golden caster sugar
1 egg
220ml milk

FOR THE CINNAMON GLAZE
½ tsp ground cinnamon
2 tbsp golden caster sugar

Put the sultanas and peel into a bowl and pour over the mulled wine. Leave to soak for at least an hour, or preferably overnight.

Preheat the oven to 200°C. Line a baking sheet with greaseproof paper.

Sift the flour, baking powder and spice into a mixing bowl, then rub in the butter until the mixture resembles fine crumbs. Stir in the sugar. Strain the soaked sultanas and peel and gently mix them in. Using a fork, mix the egg and milk together. Make a well in the centre of the dry ingredients and pour in enough liquid to make a soft dough.

Turn out onto a lightly floured surface and roll out to about 3cm thick. Stamp out using a 7cm round cutter and place on the baking sheet. Press the trimmings together, re-roll and stamp out more rounds.

Make the cinnamon glaze by mixing together the cinnamon and sugar. Brush the scones with a little of the remaining milk and egg mixture, then sprinkle the cinnamon mixture over the top.

Bake for 12–15 minutes until golden brown. Serve with clotted cream and blackberry or plum jam

49

Hughenden (BUCKINGHAMSHIRE)

The manor house at Hughenden is a real little delight of a place. I visited there because it had been the home of Benjamin Disraeli, but once there I discovered another fascinating 'bonus' aspect of its history.

Disraeli was born Jewish but his father converted to Christianity when Benjamin was twelve. He was known for spending way beyond his means, so when he got the chance to marry a rich widow he took it. Happily – albeit the wrong way round – after marrying he went on to fall in love with her, describing her as 'the most cheerful and the most courageous woman I ever knew'. As well as being prime minister, Disraeli was a novelist, and a Byron fan-boy. As you might imagine, Byron wasn't much of a role model – basically what Disraeli learned from him was how to dress extravagantly and spend excessively.

Now, on to our bonus. Hughenden is now also famous for its contribution to the Second World War. Commandeered by the Air Ministry in 1941, it became the secret centre of map production, creating the maps used for night-time bombing raids over Germany. What is astonishing is that nobody even knew about Hughenden's wartime role until 2004! For almost sixty years the story was hidden, until a National Trust guide overhead a visitor telling his grandson about how he'd sat at a desk in one of the rooms drawing maps. So now at Hughenden, as well as the Victorian layout of most of the house, go downstairs and you'll find a 1940s sitting room, complete with radio and sewing machine on the sideboard. It makes an interesting contrast.

Finally, just to show that Hughenden never runs out of surprises, in 2014 they announced they officially had the largest horse-chestnut tree in the country.

'Pumpkin Pie' Scones

Pumpkin pie is a popular dessert in North America, traditionally made in the autumn when pumpkins are in season and served at Halloween, Thanksgiving and Christmas.

500g self-raising flour
2 tsp baking powder
125g soft brown sugar
1 tsp ground cinnamon
¼ tsp ground nutmeg
100g salted butter, cubed

125g grated fresh pumpkin or canned
    pumpkin purée
1 tsp vanilla extract
25ml milk
200g condensed milk
1 egg

Preheat the oven to 190°C. Line a baking sheet with greaseproof paper.

Sift the flour, baking powder, sugar and spices into a mixing bowl. Add the butter and rub in until it resembles fine crumbs. Add the pumpkin and vanilla and mix briefly. Make a well in the centre.

Put the milk, condensed milk and egg in a jug and mix with a fork. Gradually pour the liquid into the dry ingredients, adding enough to draw all the mixture into a damp dough but not enough to make it sloppy and wet.

Turn out onto a lightly floured surface and roll out to about 4cm thick. Stamp out using an 8cm round fluted cutter and place on the baking sheet. Gently knead the trimmings together, re-roll and stamp out more rounds.

Bake for 18–20 minutes until risen and springy to the touch. Transfer to a wire rack to cool slightly. Serve warm with maple syrup and whipped cream.

50

Mottisfont (HAMPSHIRE)

What a difference 800 years makes. Today I set off on my humble little pilgrimage with the primary objective of eating Mottisfont's scones. If I'd gone there in 1214, I would have been queuing to see the forefinger of St John the Baptist. Not quite as appetising, I agree.

It seems that St John had quite a few forefingers knocking around Europe in medieval times. Back then Mottisfont was a priory, located between Salisbury and Winchester, so plenty of pilgrims would have been passing and a holy relic would have been a massive draw. However, the holy relic didn't save Mottisfont from two catastrophes: the Black Death, which struck in 1349; and Henry VIII, who dissolved the monastery here in 1536 and gave Mottisfont to his pal William Sandys.

Sandys then did something very unusual; he built a new house around the priory structure. Most abbeys were either knocked down or the building materials looted, but that didn't happen at Mottisfont. The result is that you can still see bits of the medieval priory beneath the mansion. The atmospheric cellar is stunning. And in the house itself, there are glimpses of the old underneath the relatively modern.

After Sandys, Mottisfont was owned by the Mill and Barker-Mill family before being bought by Gilbert and Maud Russell, who turned it into a country house where they could entertain artists and writers, including Ian Fleming, and other eminent people. It has some really lovely little stories: for instance, I learned that a portrait of Gilbert Russell was purchased by the National Trust using funds from their second-hand book shop.

Mottisfont has a wonderful atmosphere – the gardens and surrounding estate are large and inviting and I quite like the thought of sitting in the Whistler Room with a dry Martini waiting for dinner – or scones – to be served (*hint*).

Hot Cross Scones

A twist on a traditional Easter recipe.

500g self-raising flour
125g caster sugar
125g salted butter, cubed
75g sultanas
60g mixed peel
1 small apple, peeled and grated
1 heaped tsp ground cinnamon
½ tsp mixed spice

1 egg, beaten
125ml milk
2 tbsp apricot jam to glaze

FOR THE CROSS
35g plain flour
2–3 tbsp water

Preheat the oven to 190°C. Line a baking sheet with greaseproof paper.

Sift the flour and sugar into a bowl, add the butter and rub in until it resembles fine crumbs. Stir in the sultanas, peel, apple and spices.

Mix the egg and milk together in a jug. Gradually pour the liquid into the dry ingredients, stirring gently to make a damp dough.

Turn out onto a lightly floured surface and roll out to about 4cm thick. Stamp out using an 8cm round cutter and place on the baking sheet. Knead the trimmings together lightly, re-roll and stamp out more rounds.

To make the cross, mix the flour and water until you have a thick smooth paste. Use a piping bag with a small nozzle to pipe a cross onto each scone.

Bake for 18–20 minutes until risen and springy to the touch.

Warm the apricot jam, rub through a sieve, then brush over the scones. Transfer to a wire rack to cool slightly. Serve warm with butter.

Property Addresses

A la Ronde Summer Lane, Exmouth, Devon, EX8 5BD

Acorn Bank Temple Sowerby, near Penrith, Cumbria, CA10 1SP

Anglesey Abbey, Gardens & Lode Mill Quy Road, Lode, Cambridge, Cambridgeshire, CB25 9EJ

Attingham Park Atcham, Shrewsbury, Shropshire, SY4 4TP

Avebury Near Marlborough, Wiltshire, SN8 1RF

Baddesley Clinton Rising Lane, Baddesley Clinton, Warwickshire, B93 0DQ

Bodiam Castle Bodiam, near Robertsbridge, East Sussex, TN32 5UA

Brownsea Island Poole Harbour, Poole, Dorset, BH13 7EE

Chartwell Mapleton Road, Westerham, Kent, TN16 1PS

Clouds Hill King George V Road, Bovington, near Wareham, Dorset, BH20 7NQ

Dunham Massey Altrincham, Cheshire, WA14 4SJ

Dunwich Heath and Beach Dunwich, Saxmundham, Suffolk, IP17 3DJ

Dyffryn Gardens St Nicolas, Vale of Glamorgan, CF5 6SU

Finch Foundry Sticklepath, Okehampton, Devon, EX20 2NW

Giant's Causeway 44 Causeway Road, Bushmills, County Antrim, BT57 8SU

Goddards House & Garden 27 Tadcaster Road, York, North Yorkshire, YO24 1GG

Greys Court Rotherfield Greys, Henley-on-Thames, Oxfordshire, RG9 4PG

Hadrian's Wall & Housesteads Fort Near Bardon Mill, Hexham, Northumberland, NE47 6NN

Hanbury Hall & Gardens School Road, Hanbury, Droitwich Spa, Worcestershire, WR9 7EA

Hardwick Doe Lea, Chesterfield, Derbyshire, S44 5QJ

Houghton Mill & Waterclose Meadows Houghton, near Huntingdon, Cambridgeshire, PE28 2AZ

Hughenden High Wycombe, Buckinghamshire, HP14 4LA

Ickworth The Rotunda, Horringer, Bury St Edmunds, Suffolk, IP29 5QE

Ightham Mote Mote Road, Ivy Hatch, Sevenoaks, Kent, TN15 0NT

Killerton Broadclyst, Exeter, Devon, EX5 3LE

Moseley Old Hall Moseley Old Hall Lane, Fordhouses, Wolverhampton,

Staffordshire, WV10 7HY

Mottisfont Near Romsey, Hampshire, SO51 0LP

Nostell Priory & Parkland Doncaster Road, Nostell, near Wakefield, West Yorkshire, WF4 1QE

Nuffield Place Huntercombe, near Henley-on-Thames, Oxfordshire, RG9 5RY

Nymans Handcross, near Haywards Heath, West Sussex, RH17 6EB

Packwood House
Packwood Lane, Lapworth, Warwickshire, B94 6AT

Penrhyn Castle Bangor, Gwynedd, LL57 4HT

Polesden Lacey Great Bookham, near Dorking, Surrey, RH5 6BD

Rufford Old Hall 200 Liverpool Road, Rufford, near Ormskirk, Lancashire, L40 1SG

Scotney Castle Lamberhurst, Tunbridge Wells, Kent, TN3 8JN

Smallhythe Place Smallhythe, Tenterden, Kent, TN30 7NG

Souter Lighthouse & The Leas
Coast Road, Whitburn, Sunderland, Tyne & Wear, SR6 7NH

South Foreland Lighthouse St Margaret's Bay, Dover, Kent, CT15 5NA

Speke Hall, Garden & Estate
The Walk, Speke, Liverpool, L24 1XD

St Michael's Mount Marazion, Cornwall, TR17 0HS

Stourhead Near Mere, Wiltshire, BA12 6QF

Sudbury Hall & the National Trust Museum of Childhood
Main Road, Sudbury, Ashbourne, Derbyshire, DE6 5HT

Sutton Hoo Tranmer House, Sutton Hoo, Woodbridge, Suffolk, IP12 3DJ

Tatton Park Knutsford, Cheshire, WA16 6QN

Tintagel Old Post Office Fore Street, Tintagel, Cornwall, PL34 0DB

Tredegar House Newport, Monmouthshire, NP10 8YW

Waddesdon Manor Waddesdon, near Aylesbury, Buckinghamshire, HP18 0JH

Wimpole Estate Arrington, Royston, Cambridgeshire, SG8 0BW

Woolsthorpe Manor Water Lane, Woolsthorpe by Colsterworth, near Grantham, Lincolnshire, NG33 5PD

Wordsworth House & Garden Main Street, Cockermouth, Cumbria, CA13 9RX

Index

Acknowledgements

Author: I would like to thank: all of the NT scone bakers across the land, especially the fantastic ones I've met in person or online; all of the Sconepals that have sent me pictures of their National Trust scones – every single one of them is appreciated; my sister, who was initially baffled by this whole project but will shortly be doing her PhD in NT scones, just as soon as one is invented; my ever-supportive parents; and finally my love and thanks to Peter, aka the Scone Sidekick.

Publisher: Thanks to NT chefs for sharing their scone secrets, especially Robert Conwell at Dunwich Heath. And to Charlotte Haydon for heroically offering to test and scale all the recipes, and to Maggie Ramsay for final tweaks.

Credits for Scone Recipes: 23 Earl Grey, Dunwich Heath; **29** Honey, Ginger & Sunflower, Sudbury Hall; **33** Maple & Walnut, Scotney Castle; **35** Wholemeal Fruit, Houghton Mill; **37** Rhubarb & Stem Ginger, Hardwick Hall; **39** Salted Caramel, Scotney Castle; **41** Wet Nelly, Speke Hall; **47** Chocolate & Marshmallow, Dunwich Heath; **49** Chocolate & Hazelnut, Scotney Castle; **51** Chocolate Orange, Goddards; **53** Triple Chocolate, Dunwich Heath; **55** Raspberry & White Chocolate, Kedleston Hall; **59** Blue Cheese & Hazelnut, Waddesdon Manor; **61** Ploughman's, Sudbury Hall; **63** Welsh Cheese & Herb, Penryhyn Castle; **65** Leek & Onion, Souter Lighthouse; **67** Stilton & Cranberry, Sudbury Hall; **69** Cheese, Spring Onion and Bacon, Packwood; **71** Shropshire Blue & Fig, Hanbury Hall; **75** Red Pepper, Onion & Cheese, Moseley Old Hall; **77** Roasted Shallot, Gruyère & Thyme, Anglesey Abbey; **79** Carrot & Coriander, Kedleston Hall; **81** Beetroot, Dyffryn; **83** Horseradish, Charlecote Park; **87** Cherry & Vanilla, Hanbury Hall; **89** Cherry & Almond, Rufford Old Hall; **91** Zesty Lemon, Kedleston Hall; **93** Orange & Cranberry, Moseley Old Hall; **95** Apple & Raisin, Wordsworth House; **97** Apple & Cinnamon, Tredegar House; **99** Lemon & Coconut, Dunwich Heath; **101** Peach, Vanilla & Poppy Seed, Sudbury Hall; **103** Blackberry & Apple, Dunwich Heath; **105** Fig, Orange & Walnut, Hanbury Hall ; **107** Apricot, Moseley Old Hall; **109** Lemon & Cranberry, Waddesdon Manor; **111** Blueberry & Lemon, Hanbury Hall; **115** Christmas Pudding, Treasurer's House, York; **117** Stollen, Dunwich Heath; **119** Mulled Scones, Anglesey Abbey; **121** 'Pumpkin Pie', Dunwich Heath; **123** Hot Cross, Dunwich Heath.